ENERGIZING
CHILDREN'S MINISTRY
IN THE SMALLER CHURCH

RICK CHROMEY

ENERGIZING CHILDREN'S MINISTRY
IN THE SMALLER CHURCH

RICK CHROMEY

Standard®
PUBLISHING
Bringing The Word to Life
Cincinnati, Ohio

Cover design by Dina Sorn at Ahaa! Design and Andrew Quach
Inside design by Dina Sorn at Ahaa! Design

Library of Congress Cataloging-in-Publication Data

Chromey, Rick.
  Energizing children's ministry in the smaller church / Rick Chromey.
    p. cm.
  ISBN 978-0-7847-2192-6 (perfect bound)
  1. Church work with children--United States. 2. Small churches--United States. I. Title.

BV639.C4C475 2008
259'.22--dc22

                                    2007046888

Published by Standard Publishing, Cincinnati, Ohio
www.standardpub.com

13 12 11 10 09 08   7 6 5 4 3 2

ISBN 978-0-7847-2192-6

DEDICATION

This work is dedicated to all the "little ones"
and to my two children, Rebecca and Ryan.

ACKNOWLEDGEMENTS

No man is an island and no book is penned from a vacuum. I am eternally grateful to those individuals and congregations that have shaped my life and ministry. I am the product of your perseverance, patience, and persistence.

I want to foremost express my gratitude to my home church family at First Christian Church in Lewistown, Montana. Many of the saints that carved my faith are now gone, but not forgotten. I wish I could name every friend who charged and changed my life, but I reserve the space for a few worthy of special commendation: Ron and Lois McConkey, Kermit Owen, Ed Pangburn, Donna Ferdinand.

I am eternally grateful for the churches, some small and some large, that have entrusted their children to my care as a part-time and full-time youth minister or volunteer. Where I let you down, I ask for forgiveness. I am a man capable of many faults and failings. Nevertheless, it is my deepest hope that your memory of me is as rich as the ones I hold of you. These congregations, in order: First Christian Church (Gillette, WY), First Christian Church (Blair, NE), Oakley Christian Church (Oakley, KS), Felicity Church of Christ (Felicity, OH), New Vienna Church of Christ (New Vienna, OH), Madeira Church of Christ (Madeira, OH), Wallula Christian Church (Lansing, KS), Kirkwood Road Christian Church (Kirkwood, MO), State College Christian Church (State College, PA), Cherry Lane Christian Church (Meridian, ID), First Christian Church (Florissant, MO), and First Church of Christ (Grayson, KY).

I would like to thank the educational institutions who've hired me to equip the next generation of children's and youth ministry leaders: Boise Bible College (Boise, ID), Saint Louis Christian College (Florissant, MO), and Kentucky Christian University (Grayson, KY). To all my students, I pray that my teaching found roots and wings in your lives.

Furthermore, I'd like to acknowledge several significant individuals and influential friends who have opened doors, guided, and guarded my life through their teaching, mentoring, or just believing in me when I didn't: Ann Rapkoch, Dan Cravatt, Richard Brown, Jack Cottrell, Bill Strother, Eleanor Daniel, Gary Zustiak, Andy Hansen, David Roadcup, Charles Crane, Charles Faber, Dan Cameron, Ron Oakes, Doug Lay, Tim Nischan, Rob Ford, Chris Yount Jones, Thom and Joani Schultz, and Leonard Sweet.

Finally, and foremost, I must thank my family. First of all, Ray and Barbara (deceased) Stingley, my grandparents who cared and showed me Jesus. Second, my dad, Richard Chromey, and mom, Barbara (and Dean) Gibbs. Third, my brother and sisters: Randy, Corinne (Deffinbaugh), and Carolyne (Beers). Last, but not least, I have been blessed with the most wonderful friend in this life, a woman who lets me be "me" and just understands. Patti, I pray the years ahead are as wonderful as the past twenty-four. Thank you for being a writer's widow and saying "yes" to life with me. To my children, Rebecca and Ryan, I am so blessed to be your dad. To see Jesus live in you makes my life complete.

I would also like to thank Standard Publishing for believing in this project, with special gratitude to Robin Stanley and Margie Redford, my editors. May the smaller churches and children's ministries who find insight, ideas, and inspiration in these pages (the result of our dreams and work) discover the grand design of God in their congregations and make an eternal difference.

CONTENTS

FOREWORD 9

INTRODUCTION 11

CHAPTER 1
SPARKS 23

CHAPTER 2
CH-CH-CH-CHANGES 33

CHAPTER 3
GOING GPS 45

CHAPTER 4
MORE POWER, DIFFERENT POWER 57

CHAPTER 5
FOOD DRIVES 73

CHAPTER 6
VOLUNTEER ON! 85

CHAPTER 7
MONEY MATTERS 111

CHAPTER 8
TEACHING WITH POWER 125

CHAPTER 9
KISS AND TELL WORSHIP 141

CHAPTER 10
REALITY CHECK 157

AFTERWORD 169

FOREWORD

Our landscape across North America is dotted with thousands of smaller churches that will never appear on any "Who's Who in American Churches" list. Their leaders will never be invited to speak or write about their "secrets to success." They are not mega or mongo or anything major. Some researches even say these churches are evidence that the Christian church in America is in decline. Is that truly the case?

Dr. Rick Chromey asserts just the opposite, and I agree. When it comes to what really matters, the church celebrity circuit doesn't seem to measure up to what these smaller churches accomplish for the kingdom of God. Smaller churches are the hands of Christ reaching into communities to love broken families and reveal Jesus to people of all ages. Smaller churches reveal the heart of Christ as they love people who are grieving, suffering, striving, thriving, or celebrating in all of life's stages.

I have known Dr. Rick Chromey for many years now—as his editor, friend, and co-trainer. And in addition to Rick's integrity, commitment, and deep insights, I have seen his heart for the smaller church. Numerous times he has advocated for their specialized needs and reminded all of us about their awesome potential. I can't think of anyone better to write this book. Rick believes in the power of small in a big way. And Rick is a practitioner who focuses on practical solutions—not irrelevant theory.

You will be encouraged and equipped as you read *Energizing Children's Ministry in the Smaller Church.*

Christine Yount Jones, executive editor of *Children's Ministry Magazine*

Introduction

> *"The kingdom of heaven is like a mustard seed, which a man took and planted in his field. Though it is the smallest of all your seeds, yet when it grows, it is the largest of garden plants and becomes a tree, so that the birds of the air come and perch in its branches."*
>
> (MATTHEW 13:31, 32)

I n the heart of Montana, there is a small church of 125 members that lies miles from opportunity, innovative resources, and helpful training. Like many smaller congregations, this church struggles to make ends meet and to service its families (which can often be lured away to larger, more active congregations in town). The church employs a youth minister, fresh out of college and with limited experience (none with children). The facilities are taxed for space and harbor few amenities—like a gym or playground—that many larger churches enjoy as attraction points.

In almost every way, this smaller congregation is gloriously average. The leaders are farmers, small businessmen, and common workers. The Sunday school teachers, who have little to no formal training in educational theory, nurture their charges in a learning philosophy rooted in tradition and pride. Many of the teachers work full-time jobs or are involved in other church activities that steal their time and talents.

It's easy to forget this church is even around.

And yet it is rather remarkable.

Smaller churches, often overlooked in a megachurch culture where "bigger is better," are extraordinary in their own accomplishments and, in proper perspective, often draw larger percentages of children than churches 10 times their size. I once worked in a smaller congregation of ninety members where nearly two dozen children (preschool through sixth grade) faithfully attended. Over one-fourth of the church's total population was kids! How many 1,000 member churches can boast that a similar percentage (250 children) will show up weekly? Many smaller churches, by ratio and percentage, are actually more effective and successful than larger, more celebrated congregations.

Many smaller congregations equip the leaders of today's church. For example, in the past three decades, this seemingly insignificant Montana congregation of 125 has sent over two dozen of its own into full-time Christian ministry, both nationally and abroad. Among them are preachers, missionaries, military chaplains, people who work with the hearing impaired, musicians, children's pastors, and Bible college professors. Even more important is how dozens of churches across the nation are blessed with lay leadership provided by the men and women who grew up in this rather forgotten church.

It's a church that's literally changed the world.

And me.

First Christian Church in Lewistown, Montana, also happens to be my home church. This congregation, a living example of Jesus' parable about the mustard seed, has proven how tiny kernels in budgets and buildings can grow into a towering tree of influence and inspiration.

KIDS MATTER!

Smaller churches are exciting places for ministry! In the past fifteen years, I've been privileged to travel from Alabama to Alaska and California to Connecticut to consult, train, and interact with churches of varying sizes, types, and denominations. I've seen some of the finest children's ministries in the country, perhaps the world. I've observed innovative programs, fascinating facilities, and creative learning environments. I've dialogued with countless teachers, children's ministers, and other leaders about how to effectively reach kids in the twenty-first century.

In the end, I know one thing is certain: growing, dynamic churches are rooted in a powerful philosophy that recognizes kids matter to God.

Conversely, the most obvious sign of a church in decline is how much it deemphasizes and devalues the children in its own congregation. Most dying (and dead) churches have few to no children.

Smaller churches, often overlooked in a megachurch culture where "bigger is better," are extraordinary in their own accomplishments.

George Barna, considered one of the church's greatest researchers and trend gurus, penned a passionate apologetic for churches to focus on children *first*. In his work, *Transforming Children into Spiritual Champions*, Barna noted that out of every hundred Americans, only forty-two will make any commitment to Jesus in their lifetime. Surprisingly, however, is that thirty-two of that forty-two will make their decision prior to age twelve. Only four will commit to Christ in their adolescent years, while the remaining six will find faith following high school.[1]

You've heard that 80 percent of people make a commitment for Christ before age eighteen? Well, the truth is 80 percent of that number decides to follow Jesus before they even leave the sixth grade! Children are the most receptive audience to Christianity. Kids matter.

What Barna discovered was something I've known for a long time (and perhaps you did too): if children don't find faith before middle school, it's unlikely they ever will. Every congregation, regardless of its size, will be accountable for the children God brought to them.

That's why we need to use our resources to energize an exciting and powerful faith in kids. A passionate faith doesn't come in a pretty box or a vacuum or by chance, and neither does apathy, boredom, or passivity. Most indifferent Christian teens have grown disinterested because of their church experiences as children. Sometimes even one moment in time can make all the difference.

Several years ago, I met a vivacious Sunday school teacher. Her story is a lesson in how a single hour can change a life—forever. A story of how faith can either fly or flee.

At eight years old, she and her older brother walked in to a Vacation Bible School across the street from their house, drawn by sounds of singing. Neither had ever attended church. "It sounded fun," she recounted.

She was immediately embraced by a kind lady who took her to class where she heard stories of Jesus for the first time. Her experience was so positive she returned the next day (and the next). In fact, she started attending Sunday school regularly and then church services, eventually committing to Christ. Later, she started teaching preschoolers.

A passionate faith doesn't come in a pretty box or a vacuum or by chance, and neither does apathy, boredom, or passivity.

"It's been over 50 years now," she said, "and that day in VBS with that teacher changed my life."

"What about your brother?" I asked.

The woman paused, and her smile faded.

She then shared that her brother's experience was quite different. He was taken to a different class that was "boring" and the teacher "hurtful." Because he didn't understand church behavior and social rules, he got into trouble. Instead of gentle correction, he experienced harsh rebukes. His Bible ignorance brought ridicule and rejection. Consequently, his first picture of Jesus was a fearful one. In the end, he was ashamed, confused, and friendless.

Her brother stayed home the next day. In fact, he never went back. He vowed never to attend church again. As tears formed, the woman said her brother kept that promise until his death.

It's the story of two lives and two different teachers. One child embraced while the other embarrassed. One child loved while the other loathed. One child found faith, love, and acceptance. The other lost faith, innocence, and connection.

Two children. Two teachers. One day in life.

One child was taught the love of Jesus and the other was taught to fear him. One child learned to love while the other learned to hate. One will inherit Heaven and the other Hell.

Two children. Two teachers. One day in life.

Children are the church of tomorrow, but we mustn't forget they're also the church of today. Their attitudes, values, theology, perceptions, principles, preferences, commitments, and decisions are all formed and forged by middle school. We must recognize a child's ability to worship and praise God *now*. We must equip and empower kids to serve in valuable ministry roles *now*. We must invite their innocence and idealism into our conversations about what is happening at church and where the church is going. As Isaiah noted, sometimes a "little child will lead them" (Isaiah 11:6).

Want to know a wonderful secret? The smaller church is uniquely shaped to allow children to be involved. Larger churches may have more money, but smaller congregations have more opportunity. In a smaller congregation, there is a place for everyone—especially children. My home church taught me that truth. By fifth grade I was an usher who distributed communion and passed offering plates. I led worship in junior high and preached as a high schooler. Many of my friends did too.

Larger congregations must segregate the children from the adults on Sunday morning. It's not wrong, but it's necessary. That's what I love about the smaller church! Children can still fit with adults. The African proverb that says it takes a village to raise a child is true, but how much more rich is a child's faith that's shaped by adults? That's why this book will feature dozens of ideas and insights on how to involve children in the church.

If you want to energize your children's ministry, the first step is to recognize children matter to God.

"Smaller Church" Defined . . .

For this work, a "smaller church" is any congregation that attracts an average attendance of **200 people or fewer** for Sunday worship. It's notable that countless churches that meet in homes, mobile trailers, schools, and hotels are probably missed in most demographic studies of smaller congregations.

This book will also refer to these congregations as "smaller" and not "small" in description. Smaller churches are adaptive, growing, changing, and moving. "Small" churches are those who have allowed their traditions, congregational size, and attitudes to create a formidable wall against becoming "larger." "Smaller churches" are hopeful and whether they grow larger under God's blessing is irrelevant. "Small" churches are pessimistic and resist growth and change.

While it's okay to be "small" in number, we are called to not be "small" in faith. Therefore, we are only "smaller" in nature. With God's power and provision, we can accomplish "bigger" things and even grow numerically into a "larger" congregation.

SMALL IS THE NEW BIG

People in smaller churches often feel outnumbered by those in larger, more dynamic churches. But according to George Barna (2003), the average congregation draws ninety people (and around 60 percent of all Protestant churches have less than one hundred in attendance).[2] According to other demographic studies, 85 percent of all churches in America are under 200 active members. Simply put, most American churches are smaller in size.

Nine in Ten Churches Are Small . . .

Even though some larger churches have been celebrated for their phenomenal growth, their combined total only represents a fraction of Christianity. The average size of a church in America is around 100, and the largest percentile of churches has an attendance of less than 50. Out of the nearly 350,000 U.S. congregations, less than 5% will ever see an attendance of more than 700.

These statistics, combined with the fact that Christianity in the United States has continued to decline over the last 20 years, tells us a lot about the importance of the small church. Each of the thousands of smaller congregations is strategically important to the overall mission of Christ in America. In fact, if every small church grew only by 1% in the next two years, **it could reverse the entire decline of Christianity in our nation,** and translate into hundreds of thousands of new converts added to the body of Christ.

Excerpted from "Church Helper" http://www.victorious.org/vcm/churchsupport.htm

In observing churches and studying church growth patterns for a quarter century, I've noted a few guiding truths:

• **The 200-barrier is a church growth reality.** Some churches may balloon to 250, but either the lack of staff or inadequate facilities will burst the growth. Few churches can hire staff and build on a typical smaller church budget and may be frustrated when they encounter this barrier. Children's leaders also feel pressure because children's ministry is widely considered the new "growth gene" for churches.

• **A church that doesn't reinvent and reproduce will eventually die, though it may take decades.** Every Sunday, seventy-five churches close their doors. Two-thirds of these congregations are church plants under ten years of age that never enjoyed more than a few dozen members. Reinvention and reproduction is rooted in visionary risk that honors tradition, grace, and unity, but abhors traditionalism, apathy, and discord.

• **A church doesn't need to be larger than 200 to be blessed by God and effective in ministry.** Bigger is not always better. Many smaller congregations are "small" because their community dynamics (rural, inner-city, multiple churches) create a smaller drawing pool. A church of 200 in a town of 500 people is a mega-church to that community.

• **Dynamic smaller churches (regardless of size) and growing churches (also regardless of size) nearly always have children's ministry as a congregational priority.** From nursery to Vacation Bible School, these programs and practices are well financed, staffed by trained individuals, and roundly promoted.

Forget "Mega" . . . It's Time for Microchurches

If the megachurch is the legacy of the Baby Boomers, the legacy of the next generations may be just the opposite—smaller churches designed to feed the need for close-knit, authentic relationships. The trend, if it is one, doesn't show up yet in church statistics. But, according to consultants and researchers, there are early indications that many new churches are being designed to stay small. "You don't see many church planters today who have their sights set on huge congregations or buildings," says Carol Childress, a researcher who carries the title of "knowledge broker" at Leadership Network, a Dallas-based think tank for innovative churches. "Unlike many Baby Boomer pastors who were set on starting and growing big churches, today's church leaders are not concerned with becoming big but rather with growing authentic disciples of Christ," says Childress, whose job it is to spot trends in church life.

Excerpted from "Make Way for the Micro Church" by Nicki Reno. To read the entire article, visit: http://www.coolchurches.com/articles/microchurch.html

VOLUNTEER VARIETY

Research also reveals that if you are a children's worker in a smaller church, you probably fit one of these four descriptions:

Marilyn, who has no formal ministry credentials, is a lay volunteer in an Ohio church. Lack of time and money keep her from attending helpful ministry workshops. The church helps all it can, but few new ideas fly in this town of 900. Faithfulness and a love for children motivate Marilyn to stick with her church of sixty.

Nevertheless, she longs for creative insight and innovative ideas to energize her work with children.

Richie is a pastor at a white clapboard and brick church of 125 members in rural Oklahoma. He doesn't have a lot of time for children's ministry, but he's young and the church is convinced that Richie can overhaul the program. Richie studied preaching in seminary, and he doesn't have a clue as to what children need.

Then there's Juanita. She's a part-time paid youth worker in Southern California. She works a forty-hour week at a local mall eatery, then gives another twenty hours to the children and teenagers in her congregation. It's not easy, and though she has attended a few children's ministry workshops in her area, Juanita still struggles with inadequacy. She wants to do more.

Finally, there's Sean, a full-time paid youth minister. Fresh out of Bible college, he works in a suburban Atlanta, Georgia, church of 125 members. He took a children's ministry class in college and enjoys working with kids, but his job description includes ministry to all age groups, birth through college. Sean has books packed with games and lessons, but what he wants is a philosophical framework. He wants to know "why" more than "how." He'd also welcome workable strategies that won't tax his time, people, or budget.

I suspect you can probably relate to Marilyn, Richie, Juanita, or Sean in one way or another. And regardless of where you fit in the mix, the ideas in this book will provide you with options to energize your smaller-church children's ministry.

NO CHURCH THE SAME

But there is one final truth to consider: *No church is the same*. It's the beauty of being a part of God's creation and kingdom. Your congregation is uniquely fingerprinted and divinely crafted by God. So just because an idea works in Winnemucca doesn't mean it'll fly in Farmington. Your church has its own rich and wonderful traditions. Some ideas may counter those rituals and that's okay. Some insights in this book might trouble, even anger you. That's also okay. I simply invite you into a conversation about children's ministry. I don't expect complete agreement.

Nevertheless, I also hope you'll take some risks. Don't be afraid to try something new that you learn in the following pages. An idea that sounds outrageous may spark success in your children's ministry. I remember one time when I frantically and furiously tried to figure out why an electronic device wasn't working. I even consulted the owner's manual. And then I realized it was unplugged. The funny thing is my wife asked me only moments earlier if it was plugged in and I flippantly dismissed her suggestion with an "Of course it is!"

So be open. The energizing of your children's ministry may be a rather simple, yet forgotten, matter (like plugging back into some basic truths and foundational forces that guide effective children's ministry).

Ultimately, I pray you find this book filled with hope for you. I can't imagine what God is waiting to do in your children's ministry (and neither can you). All I know is God loves to use the small, insignificant, unappreciated, disenfranchised, impoverished, quirky, and dysfunctional to do some of His best work.

It sounds a lot like me. And probably you too.

It sounds like another mustard seed story in the making.

Sphere of Influence
by Jim Thomas

At a Pastor's seminar, I held up two rolls of pennies and one old nickel. I asked the group which they would rather possess. Like most of us the group chose to embrace the 100 pennies. It was later that I explained the nickel was a 1930s (VF condition) nickel which had been purchased at a coin shop for $5.00. Value is not always demonstrated by quantity, sometimes it is better measured by quality or potential for value.

I had been a small church Pastor for about 3 years when I was introduced to the "Sphere of Influence" concept. In essence this model measures ministry effectiveness by the amount of influence you have in a community. Rather than looking at attendance as a measure of growth, you measure attendance in comparison to potential.

Here's a simple formula:

Target area – x number of people

Attendance – y number of people

Divide target area by attendance = Sphere of Influence

When I view my church in terms of my target area, I focus on the influence in my community. In my situation I am surrounded by towns of 200 and our target area is 2000 people in our community. Currently we average 100–120 people. That means that each week I speak to 5–6% of my community. In my previous ministry I was part of a multi-staff church averaging 400 in a community of 80,000. We only reached .05% (not even 1%) of our community. We were one of the larger churches in the area and would be considered very successful in terms of "church," but in reality I have far more impact in our rural area than I did in a city area.

When viewing attendance with this formula, it is actually possible for a ministry to be healthy while remaining numerically stagnant.

Jim Thomas, "Sphere of Influence," http://www.smallchurch.com/ 06%20Sphere%20of%20Influence.htm. Used by permission.

CHAPTER 1

Sparks

> *"When we put bits into the mouths of horses to make them obey us, we can turn the whole animal. Or take ships as an example. Although they are so large and are driven by strong winds, they are steered by a very small rudder wherever the pilot wants to go. . . . Consider what a great forest is set on fire by a small spark."*
>
> (JAMES 3:3-5)

The summer before this writing, the Idaho mountains were ablaze. Forest fires destroyed millions of acres and countless homes. Billions of dollars were spent to fight fires that were nearly all the result of just a small spark. As the high desert heat dries the mountain meadows and foothills, the smallest ember can ignite a whole forest, just as James wrote. In fact, many summer fires are caused by natural friction (metal on pavement) when a vehicle showers glowing sparks into the dry tinder, unknown to the driver.

It's a great metaphor for energizing children's ministry in your church. Effective and successful children's programs will occasionally create natural friction and heat in a congregation. Children are messy, loud, frustrating, energetic, and impetuous. Many churches miss great opportunities to explode these small sparks of irritant qualities into roaring flames of opportunity. That's why you'll never energize your children's ministry unless you're willing to take some heat. Not everyone will understand your own passion for leading the kids.

But I have to tell you that to be small is to be blessed.

Remember: small is the new big.

Whether its downsizing or reducing, small is attractive. The iPod is one of the smallest (and most successful) music players. TV now comes to a cell phone screen. Small towns near major metropolitan areas are exploding (which means they won't be small much longer).

If you want to energize your church, begin by tapping into the enthusiasm of your children.

My mentor Leonard Sweet likes to note the "both/and" cultural trends in action. The church is getting both larger (mega) and smaller (micro) at the same time, as are our cars, homes, and commutes. I have an hour commute three to four times a month to Portland, Oregon (by plane), to connect with my "home" office.

Small is the new big.

Consequently, children's ministries in the smaller church possess special and unique opportunities that larger congregations can only dream about. It's good to be small. Small is tall. Mustard seeds, sparks, rudders, and bits hold powerful possibilities. After all, as a forgotten sage once said, "Anybody can count the seeds in an apple, but only God can count the apples in a seed."

Let me also suggest that change is more fluid and easier in a smaller congregation. (We'll talk more about this in later chapters.) Imagine this scenario: It's a busy rush hour and traffic is slammed and slow. There are many alternative routes, via off-ramps, side neighborhoods, and service roads. So let me ask you: Would you rather be in a Toyota or a tractor trailer? The answer is obvious. The bigger you are, the less immediate reactions and changes you can make. Small is preferred in bumper-to-bumper traffic and "being big" can be a curse (and a traffic accident waiting to happen).

So let's consider five unique sparks that can ignite effective children's ministry in a smaller church.

THE EXCITING FAITH OF A CHILD

I love the faith of a kid. It's a can-do faith. Children possess an inner enthusiasm that inspires and encourages. Children remind us of the way we used to be: carefree, innocent, exuberant, risky, and unconcerned about failures.

Church researcher George Barna comments, "As adults, we have a tendency to memorialize things in programs and routines, frequently removing the spontaneity and enthusiasm from the activity."[1] Children can remind us of what's important. They enable adults to understand that faith doesn't have to be stale or static, but it can be dynamic and filled with wonder.

The millennial generation (born between 1982 and 1998) and the yet-to-be-labeled generation (born since 1999) are groomed within a wider cultural context to be actively involved. They prefer hands-on, experiential learning. They hunger for service opportunities. They enjoy movement in worship. They desire to make a difference in their world.

If you want to energize your church, begin by tapping into the enthusiasm of your children. Let them share in your adult worship. Release them to do ministry in your community. Inspire them to live their faith freely.

Children will make mistakes, messes, and mishaps.

But that's my point.

What does every single adult—believer and unbeliever—seek in their lives? What's the greatest cornerstone of Christian theology we all long to experience?

That's right. Grace. Amazing grace.

If your church allows children to fail and falter, drowning them with grace instead of condemnation, imagine how your adults will thrive beneath that model? A church of grace—unconditional, amazing, irresponsible, unbelievable, inexplicable, wild, and wonderful—will be a touchstone for your community.

Smaller churches, because of the intimacy and size, can create these moments of grace. Messes and mistakes are welcomed and worked out.

POTENTIAL FOR PARENT MINISTRY

A vibrant, energetic children's ministry will naturally attract adults to your church, and the most receptive adults are the parents themselves.

Two years ago, Jeremy's nine-year-old daughter begged him and his live-in girl-friend to attend her Vacation Bible School closing program. Jeremy hadn't been to church in years and felt religion was for weak people. He also felt somewhat guilty for living with his girlfriend. But his daughter persisted and Jeremy honored her request.

He hasn't missed a Sunday since.

What influenced Jeremy (and his girlfriend)—who were married in the church only a few months later—to finally attend church was not a billboard, a flyer, a TV or radio advertisement, but the pleadings of his own flesh and blood. And when Jeremy relented, he discovered the church of 135 people to be a perfect fit for him. He found acceptance, peace, and grace. The Sunday prior to his wedding, the whole family was baptized.

Many smaller churches don't realize the opportunity they hold for attracting the parents of their children. Many larger congregations have specialized ministries as attraction points (sports, motorcycles, and so on) for friend-on-friend evangelism. However, the smaller church influences more through satisfying relational connections. Many parents hold wrong perceptions about church (based upon personal bad experiences) and, consequently, it requires a rewiring (new, positive experience) to change the mind.

A CLOSE FAMILY OF BELIEVERS

Children have more contact with adults in the smaller church. They rub shoulders with them in the foyer and engage them in the hallways. In the smaller town context, it's not unusual for adults to know every child too. Children are a natural part of church life.

As a boy, I like to say I had dozens of parents and grandparents, brothers and sisters, uncles and aunts and cousins. I was on a first-name basis with almost every adult in my church. "Grandma" Lois and "Grandpa" Ron held me in a hospital room only hours after I was born. "Mom and Dad" Olson took me along when they went camping. "Uncle" Kermit drove me to youth events and "Aunt" Margaret gave me a job.

I grew up among adults who mentored my faith. I sang in the adult choir. I played Bible trivia with the senior saints. I hammered nails in the new church building. I sat with adults for Wednesday Bible studies. I washed countless communion cups and folded bottomless boxes of bulletins. And in every single activity, I was alongside an adult.

The children in a smaller church have a unique advantage to engage in close personal relationships with adults (if the adults will let them!). A key task to energizing children's ministry in the smaller church is reviving a whole "family" feel where children are welcomed and connected with adults—no matter the activity, program, event, or service.

CHILDREN TODAY, CHURCH LEADERS TOMORROW

It's a simple, yet profound, truth: smaller churches can develop better leaders from their children. Why? Because the smaller the congregation, the greater the opportunity for kids to be active *leaders*.

An unfortunate consequence of many children's ministry programs and philosophy since the 1980s has been a segregation of children from leadership in the local church. Despite a broader cultural acceptance and affirmation of children in the community, the church has largely separated children and eliminated opportunities for service and sacrifice. In larger churches, it's not uncommon for a child to go years without any direct connection with the wider adult audience (other than parents).

But when children are left out of church life, the message they hear is that they don't belong. Adults will lead adults, and certain adults will keep the kids out of the rest of the adults' hair.

When children are granted occasional opportunity to attend an adult worship or situation, they're expected to sit quietly or behave ("be seen but not heard"). Rarely, they're tossed a bone that allows them to share a song, a drama, or some other performance (suggesting a dangerous message that, in the church, you only matter if you're on the stage). But since these opportunities are so few and far between, many children grow up with a stilted view of "church" and mature into a passive "pew potatoes" mentality (sit down, be quiet).

In the smaller church, the good news is children can learn leadership skills through active participation in the life of the congregation. Smaller congregations can permit children to participate in leadership meetings (especially if they involve decisions about children's ministry). Older children can create worship PowerPoint slides and successfully serve as a tech advisors. Children can pray, share devotional thoughts and testimonies, give announcements, and serve as song leaders.

You'll rarely see children doing such things in a larger church. The smaller congregation also hungers for volunteers and can miss a pregnant possibility to release children in acts of service. If you want to energize your children's ministry, tap into a philosophy that permits children to be active leaders before they turn age eighteen!

One of the consequences of early leadership involvement by children is they will probably carry their attitude of service and sacrifice into their adult years. Perhaps the reason we now struggle for adult volunteers (especially among the under forty crowd) is we trained them (through our ministry philosophies of the 1980s and 1990s) to "be quiet, sit down, and stay put."

> *When children are left out of church life,*
> *the message they hear is that they don't belong.*

Too many smaller churches model the ministry philosophies of larger churches (separate and segregate). What we fail to understand is that our small patch of ground can potentially grow a better stalk of leaders (in fact, most megachurch pastors were raised in a smaller church) because there is better opportunity. It's an advantage smaller churches regrettably may overlook.

CREATIVE GROUND FOR NEW IDEAS

Children love novelty, innovation, and unpredictability. Barna asserts that the benefit of testing new programs with children is "the assurance that kids [will] provide honest feedback, enabling the church leaders to sharpen or forget about the program or communication."[2]

What types of ideas might a church "test" on its children? Churches can try innovative schedules for Sunday morning, creative teaching methods, or new worship songs. One older small church pastor struggled for months to understand the new church computer. After one too many frustrations, the computer was shelved for former, more comfortable technology. It collected dust until the fifth grade class found it. The kids were able to teach the adults several new tricks on the machine and enjoyed some video games too.

Few larger churches are going to allow an eleven-year-old boy to play on the church computer, let alone suggest new music for Sunday's service or offer insight about a leadership dilemma. Once again, the smaller church has the edge. Giving children significant roles in the congregation is easier because they are more visible in the smaller church. In fact, the smaller you are the more parts a child can and should play.

Furthermore, it's easier to be flexible and spontaneous with fifteen kids than with fifty. In large congregations, the organization can grow to be so big that size prevents it from enjoying much liberty. Smaller churches can quickly alter plans and change course to better respond to the needs of children. Smaller churches can be more creative with meeting times or program agendas because communication can be more direct and organic.

Think of it this way: a smaller church is like a single human body. Decisions are more organic and uniquely individual. If I want to sleep in, I sleep in. If I want to watch baseball, I watch baseball. Larger churches are actually a collection of "smaller churches" or several human bodies together. When it's two or three, creativity and innovative spirit still abounds. "Let's catch a movie" or "I want Chinese for supper." But the more people that are involved, the more decisions tighten and time delays. Every family knows the fun in finding a restaurant that suits every taste, but the bigger the family the fewer the choices.

Some may conclude that since children's ministry in a smaller church is more flexible, it should operate with little planning. They even find the idea of "winging it" attractive to meet every child's need. Why plan at all, especially if you can change on a dime?

The answer is simple: careful, thoughtful planning actually allows the children's worker to be more creatively spontaneous. The goal is defined, the needs are assessed, and the resources are accounted for. The children's leader can now creatively match needs and resources to energize an efficient, exciting program that builds faith in children. And all this work is done up front—it's planned.

No one would take a family vacation just "winging it." It would be a miserable experience. Recently our family traveled to Seattle, Washington, for a day of sightseeing. My guitar-toting teenaged son enjoys the music of Jimi Hendrix and anticipated a visit at the Experience Music Project near the Space Needle. I planned the trip thoroughly (from hotels to restaurants), but I overlooked one small detail: museum operating hours. As it turned out, the museum was closed one day a week, and, unfortunately, it happened to be the only day we were in Seattle. So even careful planning doesn't guarantee everything, but you'll find more success through planning than "winging it."

An effective children's ministry within the smaller church will capitalize upon the unique, individual strengths of being small. Leaders can energize the smaller-church children's ministry through a disciplined strategy of innovative planning that involves children and their parents and increases their leadership opportunities.

Careful, thoughtful planning actually allows the children's worker to be more creatively spontaneous.

An energized children's ministry is one that celebrates children both as the church of tomorrow *and* today. It's not "either/or," but "both/and."

The consequence of an energized children's ministry is as mighty as turning an ocean liner with a small rudder or setting thousands of acres ablaze with a small glowing ember. The power might be small, but the potential is unlimited.

It only takes a spark. You can be the one to light it.

CHAPTER 2

Ch-Ch-Ch-Changes

> "[Jesus] went on, 'No one cuts up a fine silk scarf to patch old work clothes; you want fabrics that match. And you don't put your wine in cracked bottles.'"
>
> (MATTHEW 9:17, *THE MESSAGE*)

love the church! It's always held a special place for me, especially as a kid. Fellowship dinners, ping-pong contests, perfect attendance pins, and flannelgraph memories frame my early church experience. I was weaned on fiery sermons, sword drills, two-week VBSes, and hymns.

But I'll be honest. The church of my childhood is heading into history. Like a cracked wineskin trying it's best to handle new wine, it struggles to hold its own. But most of us know that reality already. We're recognizing that something bigger than a fad or trend is shifting things around. An epoch cultural change—driven by technological revolutions—has birthed a fresh world. Global. Interactive. Image-driven. Experiential. Digital. Fluid. Connected. Tolerant. Spiritual.

Bob Dylan predicted, "The times, they are a-changin'."

Consequently, pioneering efforts to manufacture new wineskins have emerged. It doesn't mean old wineskins are wrong (for, in many contexts, they still work). Nevertheless, fewer people are drinking—whether believer or nonbeliever. In a Starbucks' world, it's hard for church coffee to compete. And that's the problem. We've got divinely-imported Jesus java (a superior blend) but tend to brew it weak, pour it in Styrofoam, and serve it lukewarm. Our coffee beans are fine. But our brewing and presentation need work.

Children's ministries, in particular, are impacted by cultural change. Kids are quite connected to their world through social networks at school, in their neighborhoods, and through organizations. Smaller churches need not resist cultural change nor fear how culture impacts children, but neither should they naively embrace every fad or trend.

"In this new world, some of us are immigrants, Some of us are natives. Not to understand this one little fact is not to make it in—if not into—the future."
LEONARD SWEET (LINER NOTES TO *CARPE MAÑANA*)

A NEW WORLD HAS COME . . .

Every several hundred years, a massive cultural earthquake hits that levels the previous world and establishes new rules, new norms, and new perceptions. Such cultural shakings tend to be rooted in unique technological innovations that alter how a culture interprets, communicates, and operates. Business guru Peter Drucker once stated,

> Every few hundred years in Western history there occurs a sharp transformation. Within a few short decades, society rearranges itself—its worldview; its basic values; it's social and political structure; its arts; its key institutions. Fifty years later, there is a new world. And the people born then cannot even imagine the world in which their grandparents lived and into which their parents were born. We are currently living through just such a transition.[1]

Certain technology has the power to rearrange our world's perspectives or, in the words of Thomas Friedman, to create a "flat world." For example, television moved us from a "word" (Gutenberg) culture into an "image" world. The cellular phone and Internet flattened communication and heightened a relational desire to connect anytime, anywhere. The Web and television engineered an experiential culture where truth is discovered via the senses.

Leonard Sweet notes how the Internet, in particular, has changed the world:

- from manual (radio, TV, typewriter, film) to digital (computers, faxes, cell phones, and www)

- from linear ("straight, cause-and-effect") to loop ("hopscotch, hyperlink")

- from word (literature) to image (audio visual)

- from vast ("big and small") to fast ("fast and slow")

- from sharp ("either/or") to fuzzy ("both/and")

- from outer space ("truth is out there") to inner space ("truth is both 'in here' and 'out there'")

- from "Clockwork Orange" (mechanistic science) to "Web Green" (organistic holism).[2]

The value of understanding new cultural languages (relational, experiential, and image) cannot be understated, especially in any attempt to energize a children's ministry in postmodern culture. We need to listen to what kids are saying, watch what they are watching, and go where they are going.

New technologies tend to impact the young, who are open and appreciative. Furthermore, the smaller church has a decided advantage in that it can learn and speak these new dialects more quickly than larger congregations.

Let's investigate four areas where our world has changed, and how smaller-church children's ministries can transform to meet these new perspectives.

UNDERSTANDING THE DIFFERENCES	
MODERNITY (1500 – 2000)	**POST-MODERNITY (2000 – ?)**
Conquest & Control	Cooperation & Community
Machine/Mechanism	Body/Movement
Science & Reason	Spirituality & Experience
Objectivity	Subjectivity
Debate & Conversion	Dialogue & Conversation
Organization	Organism
Individualism ("Me")	Group ("We")
Denominational	Ecumenical
Regional	Global
Rules	Relationship
Printing Press, Telescope, & Clock	Internet, Cell phone & TV
Time-based, Seat-Based	Timeless, Wall-less
Church is a "club"	Church is a "community"
Passive	Active
Lecture, Discussion	Experiences, Dialogue
Word-Based	Image-Driven
"Land" (Leonard Sweet)	"Water" (Leonard Sweet)
Police Officer & Lawyer	Tour Guide & Artist
School & Prison	Journey & Party
Builders & Boomers (born pre-1961)	Gen X & Millennials (born post-1961)
Bible is a study (theology)	Bible is a story (narrative)
"Think outside the box"	"There are no more boxes"

FROM "CLUB" TO "COMMUNITY"

The modern church has a problem. It may be the reason our culture can misunderstand us. We've created a Christian "club" (within a deeper "Christian" subculture) where membership is everything. Once inside, our rules, rites, and rituals define and distinguish. Fish symbols and crosses. Coded prayer language. Christian-ese dialects. From baptism to communion, we sing, pray, and kneel.

Learn the rules, shake hands, and go home. When children learn these codes of conduct, they do what's necessary to get "in" the club and then they disappear. Faith becomes a game, not a life-changing experience.

In the old world, a club mentality made sense. Liturgy, structure, passivity, and membership were normal. Institutions (business, entertainment, education) created clones and clubs. In a cookie-cutter world, where misfits were marginalized, the club idea worked well. Remember the *Titanic*? First class, coach, and steerage. Modern Christianity preached to "be in, but not of, the world" (which meant exclusivity, doctrinal purity, and rites of passage). Consequently, the church culture adopted many nonbiblical inclusive rules to funnel proselytes through proper dress, music, or other lifestyle codes (resulting in legalism). Church leaders evolved into CEOs, presidents, and judges.

RESOURCES SPOTLIGHT

Check out these authors to read more about how today's worldview is affecting the church.

Tony Jones (*Postmodern Youth Ministry*)

Dan Kimball (*Emerging Church, Emerging Worship*)

Brian McLaren (*Adventures in Missing the Point, The Church on the Other Side, A New Kind of Christian*)

Leonard Sweet (*SoulTsunami, A Is for Abductive, Aquachurch, Carpe Mañana, Post-modern Pilgrims*)

Robert Webber (*Ancient-Future Faith, The Younger Evangelicals*)

But "members only" clubs are now dying beasts (e.g., the Moose or Elks). The Masonic Lodge, even with its altruism and philanthropy, has flatlined. What's replacing them? Communities. The Internet has transformed "clubs" into "communities" with minimal membership rules. EBay advertises as an auction community. Yahoo! is an online mall where people gather to dialogue their hobbies, interests, or lifestyles. Chat rooms and instant messaging create immediate community. Fantasy sports have single-handedly transformed professional sports. The most popular events are community-rich: spring-break getaways, motorcycle rallies, or Super Bowl parties. A popular new trend is "flash mobs," where a group gathers to hawk a product or protest an idea before a camera.

What's this mean to a smaller-church children's ministry? Simple. We need to creatively and boldly confront culture to help children develop powerful, personal relationships. Cyber community is good, but deep (and pure) relationships are better. Children's church is an excellent place to encourage and explore personal testimonies. It's also time to creatively rethink how children's ministry can become a 24/7/365 sanctuary for prayer, communion, meditation, and connection (possibly using social networking on the Web). A recent trend has been toward multisite, multiday, and multistyle ministry. Obviously a smaller church has limitations, but could we transform VBS into a year-round event (multiday)? What if we held an all-night VBS lock-in (multistyle)? Have we even considered a totally online VBS (multisite)?

FROM "RULES" TO "RELATIONSHIPS"

Modernity loved rules. The Enlightenment (science and reason) invoked a world of sound structures. The church—seeking relevance to moderns—took on fixed formats. Service orders and three-point sermons became both time-based and seat-based. The sciences of biblical interpretation (hermeneutics) and apologetics were enthusiastically embraced. We propagated laws and principles, from salvation to learning to church growth. Theologians (using deductive reasoning) boxed up God for future dissection and discussion, literally stripping Divinity of His Mystery and Majesty. Dissenters were labeled, disfellowshiped, or isolated, creating divisions and denominations.

> *We need to creatively and boldly confront culture to help children develop powerful, personal relationships.*

Megatrend author John Naisbitt rightly predicted a "high tech" world unleashes "high touch" opportunities. Naisbitt defines *high tech* as "future advancements, innovations, progress" that control and create recognition of "all that is greater than we."[3] Essentially, it's rejecting the intrusion of technology for simplified lives that "preserves our humanness."[4] Ultimately, technology produces a culture that Naisbitt argues is "spiritually empty, dissatisfying, and dangerous."[5]

Wireless and visual technologies fuel relational hunger. Cell phones, e-mail, and BlackBerrys instantly connect and create immediate emotional need (just watch how everyone scrambles to answer their cell phones!). Reality TV is a window into relationships. Messy. Goofy. Carnal. Spiritual. Reality shows reveal relational dysfunctions and unmask authentic motives and meaning, values and vices. Social networking sites like MySpace and Facebook have become standard fare.

The truth? Our culture hungers for a hug.

Quantum physics has uncovered a world of relationships, not rules. The subatomic world is chaotic, crazy, and unpredictable. Similarly, relationships are messy and disorderly—ripe with false motives, bad decisions, and poor values. This chaotic truth is tempered by a Spirit-breathed, grace-full fellowship that forgives, risks, and serves. Relationships can't be ordered, manufactured, or programmed (which explains why "small groups ministries"—even with children— often struggle to succeed).

What does this mean to a smaller-church children's ministry? Primarily, we need to resist counting "nickels and noses" as signs of success and again to rethink Sunday-only programming. Tomorrow's churches will undoubtedly resemble 24/7 spiritual "health" centers, featuring support/activity groups, crisis counseling, online biblical teaching, service learning, and experiential worship. Children's ministries might resemble a Chuck E. Cheese's, where a "kid can be a kid" and where adults are free to connect on a child's level.

FROM "WORDS" TO "IMAGE"

Image is everything.

The "eyes" have it.

Metaphor is in.

If I mention September 11, what do you see? If I say "Katrina," what comes to mind? If I name "Donald Trump," what happens? You probably see images. Towers on fire. A hurricane's devastating aftermath. A pointed finger, a bad haircut, and a booming "You're fired!"

The modern world was constructed on Gutenberg technology. Words were it. Books and libraries. Newspapers and journals. Debates and argument. For hundred of years, the modern world mass-produced words. The church, seeking cultural relevance, followed suit. The Bible was divided chapter and verse (then studied and paraphrased, ad nauseum). Hymns were ordered prose. Martin Luther sparked a reformation with *Ninety-Five Theses*. Alexander Campbell mobilized restoration through writing and debate. In a word-world, such strategies spoke volumes.

The advent of moving pictures, TV, and virtual technology created new ways to process information. Since 1960 (the first televised debate), presidential elections have hinged on image. Advertising is image. YouTube has reinvented broadcasting and everything it touches (from politics to entertainment to religion). The communicators in our culture invoke images. Stephen Spielberg. Michael Moore. Mel Gibson. The Wachowski brothers.

Children's ministries must learn to carve messages with scriptural, image-soaked metaphors. Plus, we must incorporate living images into our learning and worship experiences. Fire symbolizes God's presence. Water denotes cleansing and purity. Wind represents movement and life. Jesus is a rock, gate, shepherd, and pearl. The church/kingdom resembles a net, field, body, and bride. Postmodern communicators use stories, metaphors, and video clips to cast "eye"-deas.

The ability to create and master media will be a valuable skill in the coming decade. Images used with children to help them learn, worship, or connect should be fluid, not static; authentic not plastic. Video clips, music videos, and object lessons will find increasing acceptance for those who communicate with children. ✈

FROM "DESTINATION" TO "JOURNEY"

Today's most common cultural metaphor for life is "journey." Amazing races. National treasure hunts. Adventure vacations. Enchanting cruises. Life is a road trip filled with pit stops and potholes, accidents and incidents.

To the contrary, the modern world was about conquest and destination. Questions needed answers. Everything had bottom lines (reduce/deduce). In contrast, our emergent culture prefers confusion and doubt, investigation and inquiry. It prefers to depart, disappear, and be "abducted."[6] Homes have evolved from castles into cathedrals—sacred retreats. The hottest trend is weddings at beaches, underwater, or airborne. People are moving south and west, toward mountains and ocean.

The modern church manufactured a "field of dreams" machine. If you build it, they'll come. We framed facilities as a focus. Many children's ministries brag on their buildings, budgets, and body counts, but overlook body life. The numerical growth outweighs children's spiritual health. Seen these rules? "No soda in the children's church hall." "No tape on the floor." "No kids in the sound booth." Essentially, we want buildings and ministries free of spills, messes, goofs, and gaffes. But children are different (they're all those things). The body life (particularly with the "under-twelve" set) stinks and stutters, burps and bites, tumbles and trembles. You can't regulate life. It's messy. Stuff happens. (And usually a preteen is right in the thick of it!)

Children's ministries must learn to carve messages with scriptural, image-soaked metaphors.

Life often resembles the Emmaus disciples. Troubled and disillusioned, they trudged home with heavy hearts. Their faith was tested. Their messianic theology questioned. Perhaps they debated whether to stay connected to the Jerusalem believers. Maybe they were thinking of packing it in.

And then he shows up (only they don't recognize him). The stranger walks and talks, listens and learns. He lets them unload the emotional baggage. He embraces their doubt. No masks. No tricks. He explains Scripture. Finally, in a moment of deep communion, the Master reveals his identity (then disappears again!).

I don't get it. They walked miles with Jesus and didn't know it was him. They conversed with him and didn't recognize him. They witnessed his miracles and still doubted. Jesus even lets them sulk and hides himself. It's messy, murky, and I love it. Life is lived out of darkness and doubt, trial and tests.

Consequently, children's ministries should guide and guard faith. We are the spark that sets a child's faith aflame. We don't have all the answers. In fact, it's better that we don't. We just walk with the kids along the road. We provide for their needs and protect them from evil. We create experiences that encourage growth rather than lecture halls that stifle. We are "tour guides," not "cops." This is a clear advantage for smaller-church children's workers who can have significantly deeper and more intimate relationships with children.

NEW WINESKINS . . .

In Jesus' day, new wine was naturally poured into a fresh and flexible wineskin so when fermentation caused the wine to expand, the skin—often made of animal bladders—grew with it. Old wineskins were hard and unbending, allowing no opportunity for expansion (which is why they'd crack and leak). New wine demanded new wineskins.

It's a great image for how the church must respond to culture.

We must continually pour our message (the gospel) into containers that are culturally relevant. The other night I watched a teen speaker use a video clip from the *Titanic*. For me, that movie was released just yesterday, but it wasn't. The *Titanic* was a blockbuster in 1997! The majority of this teen speaker's audience was between four to eight years old when that movie was released. Do you see my point? For children, if you're using examples (clips, stories, metaphors) more than two years old, you're pretty much irrelevant. As I write this sentence, children are fans of Hannah Montana, the Cheetah Girls, and Harry Potter. They're playing *Guitar Hero* and Wii. Preteens are blogging at zoomshare, surfing to YouTube, and creating online profiles in social networking sites. These are cultural reflections that reveal a relational, experiential, and image wineskin. Few churches recognize how deeply these media magnets can influence children's values, choices, and thinking. Even worse is the fact that by the time you read these words, many of these cultural icons will be "so yesterday."

Face it, wineskins age quickly. It's one of the reasons I love working with children. It's hard to grow too old if you stay culturally relevant. Children's culture keeps you young.

We must continually pour our message (the gospel)
into containers that are culturally relevant.

Ultimately, every wineskin will be unique. That's because every part of the body looks different. Every smaller church is different. Every kid is different. Certainly, authentic emergent ministry will be creatively contextualized to geography, social need, and cultural bridges. No single wineskin fits all.

That's why I love the church!

It's big enough for everyone, including you and me.

Especially you and me.

And our children.

CHAPTER 3

Going GPS

> *"I went to Jerusalem, and after staying there three days I set out during the night with a few men. . . . I went up the valley by night, examining the wall. . . . Then I said to them, "You see the trouble we are in: Jerusalem lies in ruins, . . . Come, let us rebuild the wall of Jerusalem."*
>
> (NEHEMIAH 2:11, 12, 15, 17)

'm a sucker for new technology, especially stuff that tempts my desire to do things faster, farther, and finer. I'm not a "first adopter," so you won't find me camping out at Best Buy for the latest techno-gadget, but I do suffer from "techno-lust" and will eventually satisfy my hunger, whether it's an iPod, BlackBerry, or wireless Bluetooth hands-free headset (most of which will probably be old-school tech when you read this paragraph!).

A few years ago, I upgraded a rental car with GPS (Global Positioning System). I was immediately captivated by the device, especially the calm audio instructions to "turn right in one mile" or "you have arrived at your destination." Occasionally, I'd test the gentle gal in the box by intentionally missing my turn, only to be given secondary instructions which led me to return to my proper route. Funny, she never yelled at me.

The GPS knew where I was (and wasn't), where I needed to go, and how to get me there. Wouldn't it be great if every children's ministry possessed a similar device wired into their collective consciousness? Imagine how easy it would be to remain focused to congregational values and visions.

Nehemiah understood the importance of intentional purpose-driven work. As a cupbearer to King Artaxerxes, Nehemiah was in a comfortable, secure leadership position. But when he learned that Jerusalem's wall was in ruins, he was moved to tears and sought permission to lead the rebuilding. Prior to this massive remodel, however, Nehemiah carefully evaluated the situation and tapped into a God Positional System to effectively focus his work towards a divine mission.

Nehemiah's leadership is a model to smaller church leaders—especially those who work with children. Nehemiah never let his passion to rebuild trump crafting a common vision. He walked the entire perimeter of the wall, inspecting every crack and crevice. Similarly, it's crucial for smaller-church children's leaders to survey the entire program (noting strengths and weaknesses) with a view towards focused and purposed improvement.

VALUING EVALUATION

Effective evaluation of a ministry covers every aspect of a ministry, including curriculum, teachers, the results desired, the learner's experience, facilities, equipment, and how the overall program is administrated and organized. Evaluation also includes a purposeful survey of the congregational children as well as kids on the fringes or in the neighborhood. Effective evaluation aids planning strategies that truly impact targeted audiences.

A thorough evaluation can reveal resources previously unknown, including willing adults just waiting to be employed in children's ministry. It can also uncover equipment, ministry resources, and teaching materials long forgotten. Several years ago, I took a college Christian education class on a tour of a local smaller church. As we traveled deep into the basement, the children's minister led us to a forgotten locked closet. After fumbling to find the right key, the door was opened and inside was a treasure chest of prizes, teaching aids, games, videos, and even old candy. Many of the items were still useful, providing a serendipity moment for the leader with the key!

A complete evaluation may expose programs that require drastic changes or worse. Ending or revamping a program may spark discouragement to the leaders involved, and it may even invoke anger and combative consequence. Nevertheless, a children's ministry properly focused around a common vision will succeed over inferior plans laid outside the purposed parameters.

Evaluation also reveals what you're doing right. You might discover that your curriculum plan is meeting needs and building biblical knowledge in the lives of children. Or that you've got well-trained, gifted teachers and leaders. You may find that a program is doing an excellent job of attracting new families to your church. Evaluation affirms your successes and allows you to build on programs already working well.

Effective evaluation aids planning strategies that truly impact targeted audiences.

A final advantage is that evaluation allows children's ministry to better plan for the future. When you know exactly how things are going in your ministry, you'll be able to compare your present program to the needs of the congregation and the community. Evaluation helps a smaller-church children's ministry look forward with confidence. And the more comprehensive the evaluation, the better your chance for success. It's like having a GPS with you everywhere you go. No matter what happens, you can always steer your children's ministry back to its proper direction.

WHY CHURCHES DON'T EVALUATE

Smaller congregations usually don't evaluate, often considering the task unnecessary. It's one of the reasons they fail to grow or have improved situations. Assessment implies a future-focus and many smaller church leaderships believe that looking forward wastes energy better suited for today's needs. To those people, evaluation and planning indicate a lack of trust in God. One small church leader told me "Jesus said not to worry about tomorrow," and he's right, to a point. Contextually, Jesus was speaking to individuals and not a church though. Later Jesus speaks to collective leadership about building a tower and clearly calls for estimation and evaluation first, before laying a single brick (Luke 14:28). Through evaluation and planning, a smaller church energizes itself around a cost-effective, life-changing purpose.

So why don't smaller churches evaluate their ministry to children?

• **Time.** Proper evaluation takes time, and because smaller-church children's leaders are already wearing so many hats, evaluation can eat up time that seems better invested elsewhere. Besides, it's easier to evaluate informally (that is, to allow situations to create consequential evaluation for improvement). One small church never viewed an organized budget as necessary. "We just pay the bills as they come," an old deacon confessed. Unfortunately, without a budget, there was also little planning (because everything desirable carried a price tag and most were seemingly out of reach). Ultimately, the bills got paid, but any vision for improvement and change in this church died on the vine.

• **Resources.** Smaller churches almost always need resources, and evaluation costs money. Assessment tools, especially paper surveys, can quickly add up in time (to review) and money (to print). Sometimes a smaller church will have the proper resources, but procrastinate. Several years ago a small church noticed a damp spot (with minor dripping) in its sanctuary. The matter was discussed and then tabled at the next board meeting because more pressing issues were at hand. In time, especially after every hard rain, the condition worsened (but unless it was a Sunday, no one was impacted) and since the cost to fix it kept rising with each worsening, the ceiling was left alone while temporary patches were applied. Until one night one final hard drenching rain collapsed the whole side of the church roof. What was once a $100 fix was now a $10,000 repair that impacted worship services for several weeks.

Resources will always be an issue in the smaller church. And yet, effective evaluation can actually save money and time.

• **Fear of Failure and/or Change.** Too often smaller-church children's workers are afraid to change because they fear failure. And since it's an evaluation that almost always produces the need for change, the guiding philosophy is "don't evaluate." This head-in-the-sand approach might satisfy some, but ultimately it creates larger consequences that impact the many.

Even when proper evaluation takes place and changes are made, there's a chance that the changes won't work. Many smaller congregations introduce change too quickly, without sufficient facilities, equipment, finances, or volunteer support. As noted already, just because it's easier for a small church to make a rapid U-turn in rush hour traffic, doesn't mean it's the right route. Too many changes implemented too quickly (something larger churches avoid simply because of their size) can actually be more detrimental, even destructive, in the end.

Smaller churches must allow time for big changes to take root. That includes giving the congregation some time to get used to the change. If the congregation members can see the potential for positive results, they'll work through the change, even if it's uncomfortable at first.

> ## TEACHER EVALUATION
>
> **T**—Temperament? (personality, attitude)
>
> **E**—Engaging? (learner involvement)
>
> **A**—Appearance? (grooming)
>
> **C**—Creativity? (innovation)
>
> **H**—Heart? (desire to learn/teach)
>
> **E**—Expertise? (knowledge of subject)
>
> **R**—Readiness? (preparation)
>
> For more evaluations of classes, teachers, and instructions, check out "The Sunday School Page": http://sschool.com/content/eval/evaluation.htm

MAKING EVALUATION WORK

Effective evaluation isn't rocket science, but it does have a few helpful guidelines:

• **Keep it simple.** A well-designed half-page survey for each group will reap a better response than a five-page questionnaire.

• **Survey everyone.** Include children, parents, church leaders, the janitor, and anyone else involved with the church.

• **Evaluate your entire children's program regularly.** Evaluate curriculum, facilities, teachers, classroom experiences, specific programs (VBS, Sunday school, children's church, choirs, camps, events, and so on), and children's attitudes. It's wiser to evaluate on a regular basis, little by little, than to undertake a huge annual assessment. If your program is evaluated after a rough season, it may make the whole year look worse. As a college professor I always found it ironic that class evaluations were distributed one week before finals, when a student was raging with fear, negativity, and questions.

• **Keep your evaluations low-key.** If you're assessing a teacher or classroom experience, ask the teacher if he prefers to be taped or personally evaluated. Explain why you are doing the evaluation and the benefits that can be gained from such an evaluation. Some churches now incorporate hidden cameras in their classrooms to root out any abuse, poor teaching practices, or learning issues. This inexpensive technological solution, however, may be met with stiff resistance (although it could be rightly argued that hidden camera recordings, ultimately, protect teachers from unfair accusation). Most competent teachers will have no problem with evaluation (hidden, taped, or otherwise). Those who resist may be the ones who need to be watched the most.

RESOURCES SPOTLIGHT

Personality Sorter

Matching personalities and releasing people into ministry can be difficult, but an effective, free online personality temperament sorter can be found at www.keirsey.com (follow the link for "Keirsey Temperament Sorter II"). For a few dollars, a complete analysis of each person can be created.

This sorter is remarkable in understanding various personalities on a team and how a leader can maximize potential.

• **Don't be secretive about the results.** Let people know what you discover, and they'll be better able to understand why you make changes.

• **Maintain the privacy of individuals.** If respondents are allowed to give their opinions anonymously, you'll probably get more accurate assessment of attitudes. Nevertheless, extreme care should be taken to prevent free-flowing, unfair, and irresponsible criticism. A negative critique of a program is helpful, but if it degrades a person (right or wrong), it's useless.

• **Learn from others.** A simple evaluation of other churches in your area might help you to discover unmet needs that your church can address. Visit another children's program on a Sunday morning. Ask a friend what her church does for midweek children's programs. Attend another church's Vacation Bible School for a night. However, remember in the final analysis it's not healthy to rate your ministry's effectiveness on the basis of what others are doing. Measure yourself against your own program objectives and goals.

• **When you can't survey everyone, survey a representative sample.** A successful survey will provide a snapshot of your ministry and will reveal potential dangers. To get accurate results, try to survey a cross section of respondents that truly represents your congregation.

• **Encourage participation.** Consider how many people will actually return your questionnaires. If one person in three participates, you'll have a good picture of attitudes, perceptions, and suggestions.

Proper evaluation takes work. But it's much better to conduct regular evaluations and to fix small problems than to plunge your head into the sand and ignore what's going wrong. Ignored problems never go away; they just get bigger.

POSITIONING YOUR CHILDREN'S MINISTRY

A global positioning system that redirects, reorients, and restores a children's ministry to a proper place or purpose would be worth its weight in gold. Nevertheless, it is possible to incorporate a GPPPS to effectively evaluate your smaller-church children's ministry: Glance, Ponder, Point, Plan, Survey.

• **G—Glance.** A glance is more than a glimpse. It's a purposeful and yet brief study of the surroundings and situation. It's a short observation of what's happening. Similarly, every evaluative tool should be short yet substantive; a glance merely to glean a body of information for further study, attitudinal perspective, or strength/weakness. Glances aren't stares. They don't threaten or create fear. A glance simply connects, pulls in relevant information, and then looks away.

Example: A three-question survey for parents that they deposit in the offering plate. Three questions: What grade would you give our children's ministry overall (A=Outstanding; B=Very Good; C=Fair; D=Poor; and F=Failing My Family)? What is your greatest concern about the children's ministry in our church? What is one suggested improvement we could make?

• **P—Ponder.** Once enough relevant and useful information has been collected (it may take various glances), the next step is to reflect on what you have found. Study your findings and create some initial conclusions. You may discover that children's attitudes (good or bad) about a particular teacher are strong. You may learn that a few classrooms are insufficient for the groups that meet in them. You may conclude that you'll need additional resources in the coming year.

Example: A noticeable concern of the parents was a lack of supervision for events. Several parents complained that children were getting hurt at events.

• **P—Point.** Once you have made some firm conclusions, it's time to refine and focus your direction. At this level, decisions are made and vision is cast. Now that you know you have weak teachers, what's next? How will you help them to improve? Now that you realize some classrooms are inadequate, how will you repair or remodel them? Now that you recognize insufficient resources, what solution will resolve the problem? It's at this point that you create a guideline, a rule, a purpose, and a direction.

Example: A policy is created that demands certain ratios of leaders to children for every event.

• **P—Plan.** Once you recognize your direction, you can now plan the trip. At this stage, a detailed response is crafted that answers the comments, concerns, or criticisms. It's an outline, a calendar, an objective, a proposal, a scheme, or a method. It's putting feet on the thinking or wings to the beliefs. It's creating a deliberate change in direction.

Example: The upcoming lock-in for 4th–6th graders will be limited in attendance, depending on the number of adults who volunteer to help with the event. This will be reflected both in advertising and a letter to all parents of regular attendees. Parents will be invited to volunteer as lock-in staff.

• **S—Survey.** The final step is to assess the plan and evaluate the proposed change. Were the improvements significant or did the situation worsen? Effective evaluation is ongoing in nature. It constantly appraises, critiques, rates, values, calculates, gauges, and reckons.

Example: After the lock-in, there was a positive response from parents overall, plus there were much fewer incidents and accidents reported among the children. A few parents who served as staff have expressed a desire to volunteer for other events. Overall, it was a safer and more productive event. The policy will stand and be expanded to other areas, as needed.

In children's ministry it's easy to lose your way, get off track, miss a turn, or get stuck. A GPPPS system will always guide you back. Smaller churches especially need to develop effective evaluation strategies to ensure quality Christian education, protect resources and teachers, and craft future plans that reflect the congregation and community. An energized children's ministry is rooted in effectual assessment of program, staff, and philosophy that's firmly supported by prayer.

You can't get anywhere without a map, but more importantly, you won't succeed without a clear assessment strategy. It's your GPS.

Goal Positioning System.

God Purposed Schematic.

Good Practice Standard.

"You have arrived at your destination."

CURRICULUM EVALUATION

An overall evaluation of your church's curriculum (all ages) should occur at least every five years. Most publishers will provide complimentary samples of curriculum to interested individuals.

Here are several questions to consider when evaluating curriculum:

- Is it biblically/theologically sound?

- Is it age-appropriate and relevant to learners?

- Is it comprehensive in scope?

- Is it balanced? sequenced?

- Is it flexible?

The MEAT of Your Curriculum

Take time to evaluate the curriculum you are using for its M-E-A-T:

Message (doctrine)

Expense (cost)

Applications (uses with learners)

Teacher-Friendliness (ease of use)

CHAPTER 4

More Power, Different Power

> *"But the* LORD *said to Samuel, 'Do not consider his appearance or his height, for I have rejected him. The* LORD *does not look at the things man looks at. Man looks at the outward appearance, but the* LORD *looks at the heart.'"*
>
> (1 SAMUEL 16:7)

What does *more* mean to you? more numbers (quantity)? improved effectiveness (quality)? additional resources? What does *more* mean in our consumer culture? For most Americans it means accumulating more possessions, power, or prominence. A bigger paycheck. More floor space. Larger attendances. We also view "more" from a qualitative perspective. We want more "bang from a buck." Better gas mileage. A nicer paint job.

The exact term *more than* appears eighty-seven times in Scripture *(NIV)*. Depending on the context, many of these are quantitative or qualitative in nature. In Luke 8:8, Jesus notes how good soil produces "more than" a hundred times better, and Mark 14:5 describes a situation where the disciples rebuke a woman who wasted oil that was worth "more than" an annual salary. These are quantitative in nature. Jesus claimed we were worth "more than" many sparrows (Matthew 10:31) and fingered a widow who gave "more than" all others (Luke 21:3). Both of these are qualitative in nature.

And yet there is a third way to interpret "more than."

Essentially, it's to *be different.*

When Jesus challenged his followers to possess a righteousness that exceeded the religious leaders of his day, he wanted them to be "different." For example Jesus said, "If you greet only your brothers, what are you doing *more than* others? Do not even pagans do that? (Matthew 5:47)" Do you hear the difference? Yes, there can be both a quantitative and qualitative element to this variance, but it's much more than a number or an improved situation. Jesus wanted his followers to be "more than" disciples. Different. Unique. A cut above.

Smaller churches and their children's ministries must learn this perspective.

Too many times we view success as nickels and noses. Or we think our programs will attract more people if we create a better environment, improved seating, or additional staff. But we miss the point, not to mention the opportunity.

Be different.

In 1997, Steve Jobs returned to Apple computers to assume a company that was on the brink of bankruptcy. Computer mogul Michael Dell sent Jobs an e-mail that callously called to "shut [Apple] down."[1] Despite trendy features, Apple computers just never succeeded in toppling the Bill Gates Microsoft empire. In 2001, a full four years after Jobs assumed control, Apple still owned only a 4% share of all computer sales in America.[2] Maybe Dell was right.

But change was already in the wind. Back in 1998, Jobs realized that Apple's products couldn't be made any better (qualitative) and there was no need to make any more (quantitative). Consequently, he challenged the Apple community to re-brand itself and to "Think Different." Jobs noted "that people had forgotten about what Apple stood for, including the employees."[3]

When Jesus challenged his followers to possess a righteousness that exceeded the religious leaders of his day, he wanted them to be "different."

Apple pursued a "more than" and "different" perspective. Steve Jobs wanted to create cool, "different" Apple-branded products that were grounded best within an Apple/iMac frame. Initially, Jobs wanted exclusivity, but eventually he relented to allow Microsoft users to enjoy the iPod. ("If they love it, they'll want to see the rest of the Apple products," admitted Jobs[4]). His willingness to concede totally changed the world. The first iPod was launched in October 2001 and a year and a half later, iTunes opened with 200,000 songs. Now you have Nanos. Video iPods. And the telephone titan iPhone.

By mid-2006, more than 58 million iPods were sold, and Apple now controls more than 87 percent of the digital download market. For Apple, it all started by a recommitment to being "different."

Smaller-church children's ministries can learn several lessons (all which energize) from Steve Jobs and the Apple story:

⊙ Failure isn't fatal (so keep swinging).

⊙ Think different—not always bigger or better.

⊙ Embrace uncertainty.

⊙ Never forget your purpose or values.

⊙ Never let the critics—even within—dictate your mood, method, or mission to grow your children's ministry.

- Find one thing and do it with excellence, rather than repeating mediocre results.

- It only takes one small thing to turn everything around.

THE SMALLER-CHURCH GOLIATHS

As a smaller church, you often face formidable foes much stronger and bigger than you are. Like David, we stand before these giants. Nevertheless, every "Goliath" has a weakness and through creativity, values, and sweat, you can bring the obstacle to its knees.

David wasn't concerned about what other people thought or what he couldn't do. Instead he concentrated on what God could do through him.

Here are a few of the more common giants you've probably already battled:

• **Volunteers.** Smaller churches routinely suffer from a volunteer shortage and struggle to effectively staff programs. The 20/80 rule is well-worn: 20 percent of the people will do 80 percent of the work. Chapter 6 will provide helpful antidotes to handling this giant.

• **Money.** Smaller churches naturally have tight budgets. In children's ministry that means walking away from some good (and spendy) programming. This ugly giant casts a long shadow that can quickly spread apathy, angst, and even anger. Chapter 7 will offer solid suggestions for succeeding on a low- or no-budget affair.

• **Attendance.** Numbers are a continual source of disappointment and discouragement in the smaller church. Enthusiasm wanes when we focus our minds on raw numbers, pure data, and plain statistics. Low turnouts. Poor attendance. Or worse, nobody shows. If you're not careful, you'll start to focus more on who's not there than the faithful few that ultimately show. The key? Don't count the kids. Make the kids count.

• **Facilities and Space.** The lack of space is a huge obstacle, especially in children's programming. Children need as much as four times the space as an adult. Many smaller churches put children in "leftover" space such as hallways, storage rooms, and even attics. That's when this obstacle presents particular problems. The answer is creative alternatives that expand walls and open new space. In one church, an odd-shaped, rarely-used choir room behind the baptistery was just a big storage area until a creative children's pastor reinvented it into a much-needed classroom.

• **Envy and Comparison.** Contentment is hard to find in many smaller congregations and if you're not careful, this giant can finish you off. It's easy to be envious of better facilities, bigger budgets, and larger churches. Sometimes smaller churches even criticize and condemn larger, more effective congregations as "selling out" or "watering down" the message. The problem is if you're always looking at what another church has, you'll miss what God has given you. Maybe the reason you don't have more is because you haven't been faithful with what you've got. Envy and comparing your situation to another only opens the door to gossip and griping, discord and division.

BECOMING A DAVID

The story of David, the shepherd boy, has always intrigued me. I've often wondered what his mother thought as he sat down for supper and boasted about knocking off lions and bears (oh my!). Or how his dad felt when Samuel anointed David king of Israel. Or what his older brothers whispered when the diminutive David refused to wear Saul's armor and walked out alone—with a sling and a few stones—to face Goliath.

One thing is certain: David wasn't concerned about what other people thought or what he couldn't do. Instead he concentrated on what God could do through him. His youthfulness and his small stature didn't matter.

If you desire to energize your smaller-church children's ministry, then take a page from David's story. Too often we worry about what we can't do rather than seek what God can do through us. We unnecessarily weigh ourselves down as we attempt to don a larger church's "armor" in program, facility, or mission. Instead we must let our smaller-church children's ministry be itself, casting aside our fears that weigh us down and seeking solace in the Living Stone that's able to deliver us from the giants that beckon.

Here are four smooth stones that can energize people, release enthusiasm, and unlock passion in a smaller church and bring down the Goliaths that threaten and tyrannize your ministry. And remember, these are simply stones. Nothing special. But with God's hand they become omnipotent.

① GO, GO, GO!

You can't spell *gospel*, *good*, or even *God* without *go*.

It's that simple. The first stone that slays giants is moving out.

The church was meant to be missional. Like a mighty ship, the bride of Christ wasn't created for the harbor, but the open water. In fact, the worst place to be in a hurricane is at port. Ships seeking to survive hurricanes improve their chances at sea.

This is completely counter to what many smaller congregations preach and practice. Somehow we've convinced ourselves that if we provide a safe, comfortable, and even entertaining place for people to come, they will.

But they're not coming. In fact, they're leaving. The fastest growing segment in Christianity is the "formerly churched"—individuals who have grown tired of a faith framed by buildings, schedules, and programs. In a 24/7/365 world, people won't settle for a 2/1/52 faith. The churches that figure out how to sling this stone into its community and culture will knock down false perceptions and priorities.

In my observation of smaller churches, I have found very few that have a missional (go) value. Rather, they prefer a static (stay) philosophy that's more content to launch programs that draw a Christian more than a nonbeliever. Evangelism is preached to the choir, by the choir, and for the choir.

And often even the choir doesn't sing along.

THE GREAT "GO MISSION!"

The leaders of one children's church lamented the low weekly (or weakly) offerings. Every Sunday the plate was passed and the kids apathetically tossed in a dime or quarter, maybe an occasional dollar. Then the leader learned that a mission agency needed only one dollar to reproduce a Bible into the Russian language. She invited this missionary to speak to the kids and share a new challenge: let's raise money for Bibles to Russia. The children caught the vision and gave over $1,300 the first year (and even held yard sales and other fundraisers for the work).

By the way, this was no megachurch. Only a dozen kids attended this smaller church's junior worship program. A few years later, these kids actually went to Russia to serve. Most graduated and went to Bible college. I wonder why.

If you want to energize your children's ministry, just remember you must "go to grow." What do I mean? Using Acts 1:8 as a guide, it's important for children's ministries to create a missional value system that innately hungers to reach the church's neighborhood, its community, and, ultimately, people in far-off places. Children are very open to missional perspectives. They welcome opportunities to enter their neighborhoods. They enjoy sharing with the community. And they long to connect with missionaries, both national and international.

As my Christian education professor famously quipped, "Impression without expression leads to depression."

② EXPERIENTIAL LEARNING

Adults tend to teach the way we were taught.

Consequently, we concentrate on pouring biblical facts into the brains of our students without any recognition that passive methodologies (like lecture and discussion) offer little retention value. I mean, think about last Sunday's sermon? How much do you *really* remember? I've actually met preachers who couldn't recall their own sermons just days after delivery.

If you want to energize learning in your children's ministry, move toward more experiential learning techniques. Many think that if we persuade the mind it will change the heart and, in turn, we'll create new behaviors. Unfortunately, that's not true. In fact, most of what we accept and believe is forged in the furnaces of personal experiences.

The cycle looks like this:

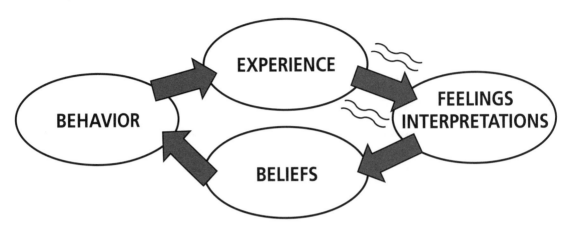

Essentially, learning starts by a personal *experience* that creates ripples of emotions and *feelings*. We feel first, think later. These feelings can be positive, neutral, or negative. However, a more intense feeling will spark more insightful thinking later. I recently attended a funeral of somebody I did not know. I went as a favor for a friend (who was a relative). The life celebration service was so inspirational, enlightening, and powerful that tears streamed down my face. My feelings were raw and intense.

Feelings, however, are only the start. What we sense or experience or feel creates *interpretations* about the experience. We frame the experience with a lens that reflects the feeling (positive, neutral, negative). At the funeral, I made several interpretations: God is faithful, even in hardship. I need to read the Word more. Life is temporary.

Naturally, these interpretations can quickly evaporate if they are not reinforced by additional experiences. In fact, an interpretation can be busted if another experience produces a more powerful feeling that contradicts it. I've actually come to enjoy funerals, especially of believers (whether I know them or not). These experiences of saints who've passed renew hope, strengthen faith, and encourage change. In time, enough similar interpretations will forge a *belief* or value.

When a belief is crafted, whatever it is, then *behavior* will follow the heart. In fact, our beliefs will influence behaviors that cause us to choose additional experiences that confirm our values. That's why I chose to attend a Saturday morning funeral for a new friend.

The smaller church is the perfect arena for experiential learning.

Some will wonder where the thinking comes in this process and that's the point: the mind is constantly working throughout the cycle. The intellect is responding to the experience (even arguing against it, if it's extremely uncomfortable), designing responsive interpretations, organizing value systems, and ultimately making choices.

Children are amazingly open to experiential learning and, in fact, are exposed to it through public school and other educational venues. Video gaming is experiential. Kid-friendly restaurants and amusements are sensory too. The smaller church is the perfect arena for experiential learning. A small class naturally welcomes flexibility and "teachable moments" (interpretations) that make active learning incredibly effective. And teacher-student relationships are richer when a class is small. Ultimately, the goal of Christian education is to help children to know, love, and follow God. Experiential learning is an effective tool to reach that goal.

③ FAMILY FIRST

A third stone in the sling is greatly aided by a smaller-church situation: family ministry. The larger a church grows, the more it tends to separate people into age groups. Each additional staff person specializes and further separates his or her ministry area from the rest: children's ministry, youth ministry, singles, senior adults, music ministry, and the list goes on.

Family ministry remains a key to effectual children's ministry.

But, again, a missional approach must be adopted. Families don't come to church. Rather the church must go to families. Smaller churches tend to already be family-focused because most are comprised of just a few families. That's why a church of 50 can more easily produce a family ministry than a church of 150.

Unfortunately, too many smaller churches adopt large-church, separatist philosophy in regards to families.

One Pennsylvania church of sixty people began a Wednesday night kids' program. If ten children—between ages two and sixteen—showed up, it was a solid night. While the adults had a Bible study, the kids had their own meeting. But rarely were there enough kids to even play a game, and the leaders struggled to provide activities that would interest and fit all the kids. Talk about frustrating! Since the Sunday programming already divided the church into age-specific groups, the church could have better used Wednesday nights to create a family-friendly evening. They could have included creative opportunities for families to grow closer to God. Unfortunately, they missed the mark.

On the other hand, one smaller church in the St. Louis area engineered an exciting family ministry that also reaches (missionally) into the community. They expanded a formerly traditional VBS program into a family festival. The program—geared to reach the whole family—featured adult seminars on special issues and creative activities designed to attract and make unchurched kids feel welcomed. Bull's-eye! Giant down.

④ BE DIFFERENT
The smaller church is different.

So embrace your differentness. It's okay. It's the one stone you hold that is shaped like no other church. The smaller congregation is amazingly unique, with natural strengths and supernatural gifts that larger churches also envy!

Unfortunately, smaller churches tend to assume that what works with 1,000 people can be pared down to work with 100. But the truth is ministry by mimicry rarely succeeds. I also think it breaks the heart of a God who specializes in the special.

FAMILY FUN

Try these family-friendly fun activities:

• A family-friendly kickball game (parents vs. kids, church leaders vs. everyone else, families with A–L last names vs. families with M–Z)

A family potluck picnic in the park

• A family Bible study in a neighborhood home

Family worship Sundays (base the service around families worshiping together)

• Family portraits (take photos of families and post them in a prominent place on the church Web site or make a church directory)

Family YMCA or gym nights (public schools may rent for no/low cost)

Family activities, such as bowling, miniature golf, bicycling, video games (Nintendo Night, Wii Tournaments)

Family trips to zoos, ballparks, theaters, or local places of interest

It's easy to see how the smaller church can get caught up in ministry by mimicry. How many of these statements sound familiar?

"Everybody else has a Vacation Bible School."

"All the cool churches are using that curriculum."

"We need to hire a children's minister—that's what First Church did."

"I went to this workshop and this church does . . ."

"What we really need is a family life center."

"We need to use PowerPoint like Community Church does."

Such attitudes can cripple a smaller congregation. When you attempt to imitate, you'll irritate. You'll rub against the grain of your own resources, facilities, freedom, and opportunities.

Instead, smaller churches should celebrate their individuality. Dare to be different. Dare to be a David. Don't worry about your size and appearance, but focus your faith on God who wants to watch you succeed. Seek to reach children around you and bring them to an authentic relationship with Jesus Christ. Rejoice in your strengths! Dream big, but don't live beyond your size. A church of 60 should be a dynamic church of 60, not a church that yearns to be a church of 600.

True vision is born when we recognize our purpose and wed it to God's plan.

CREATING VISION

A smaller-church children's ministry must envision what it can accomplish through a fervent reliance upon God's power. Too many times we see the obstacles and forget this is God's opportunity. What we see as a barrier might really be God's eventual blessing. What stands before us as a problem is probably possibility in disguise. When we look with temporary eyes, we will always miss the eternal.

That's why vision is crucial to effective ministry—especially to children. It allows you to look ahead and purposely plan today for a specific outcome tomorrow. But visionary thinking isn't always easy. In 1997, Steve Jobs couldn't envision an MP3 world, let alone that his company would rise on a Nano rather than a better iMac. David had no idea how God would rescue the Israelites from Goliath. All he knew was he had a sling and stones. He also recognized Saul's armor might protect, but it could also slow him down.

George Barna, in his classic work *The Power of Vision*, outlines five deadly traps that ambush visionaries: tradition, fear, complacency, fatigue, and short-term thinking.[5] How many of these currently invade and pervade your church's consciousness? Tradition ("We've always done it that way before"), fear ("How can we afford this?"), complacency ("I don't care; my kids are grown"), fatigue ("I give up; six years and nothing changes"), and short-term thinking ("We need to pad the pews first, then we'll buy that curriculum") routinely rust the effectiveness of a smaller church.

When we look with temporary eyes, we will always miss the eternal.

Thankfully, David didn't allow tradition ("You're just a shepherd boy"), fear ("Goliath's going to kill you, kid"), complacency ("Somebody bigger and better can handle the giant"), fatigue ("It's been a long day already"), and short-term thinking ("I'll wait until I'm older") to control his thinking. David had a solid vision that looked past the traps, trials, and troubles to inhabit a faith in what God could really do. David not only knocked the giant to his knees, he cut off Goliath's head.

You might say David knew how to get "a head" in life.

He learned how to get "more."

And so can you.

CREATIVE ACTIVITIES THAT SMALL CHURCHES DO WELL

• **Mobile Sunday School.** If you have a church van or can borrow one, hold your Sunday School lessons in it on occasion. Travel to area parks or homes for special lesson activities. Use the van for discussion times.

• **Movie Madness.** Show movies on Friday nights to your community. If your church has a portable video projector, create a drive-in in your parking lot. Or hold more intimate meetings in family homes. To avoid copyright infringement, be sure you have secured proper rights to show commercial movies in public.

• **Living Life-of-Christ Tour.** Take your children on a whirlwind tour of Christ's life, using "on location" activities. Travel to a barn and talk about Christ's birth. Go to a stream (baptism), a tall building (temptations), and a hill (Sermon on the Mount). A flower garden sets the scene for Gethsemane and then a cemetery frames Jesus' death and resurrection. Take the tour in a single day or for several weeks. Travel logistics make this difficult with more than ten kids.

• **Bicycle Progressive Dinner.** This is just like the traditional progressive dinner, except the children ride their bikes between courses. This works best with a group of four to eight children who live within several blocks of one another.

• **VBS on Location.** Take your VBS "on location" this summer. Choose your location based on your overall theme. Animals? Go to a farm. Sun and surf? Head to a beach or lake. Wild West? A ranch. Baseball? Hold VBS on a diamond. Camping? Head for the woods.

• **Nursing Home Junior Pastors.** Take interested children to a local nursing home and designate two "pastors" for each room. The children will be involved at least monthly if not more, serving as prayer partners, Scripture readers, wheelchair helpers, and any other service that's needed.

Becoming a David in Your Children's Ministry

Using the four smooth stones below, brainstorm what you can do to energize people, release enthusiasm, and unlock passion in your children's ministry.

1 Go, Go, Go!

2 Experiential Learning

3 Family First

4 Be Different

Remember, these are simply stones. Nothing special. But with God's hand, they become omnipotent.

CHAPTER 5

Food Drives

> *"Anyone who lives on milk, being still an infant, is not acquainted with the teaching about righteousness. But solid food is for the mature, who by constant use have trained themselves to distinguish good from evil."*
>
> (HEBREWS 5:13, 14)

I enjoy food. I'm especially fond of Italian (lasagna, manicotti), but I have also learned to love authentic Mexican (enchiladas) and Chinese (sweet and sour chicken with crab rangoon). My sweet tooth sometimes gets the best of me, especially if it's cheesecake, chocolate, or ice cream (mix those three and I'm headed for a sugar high). And nothing's better than a hearty cheeseburger with a side of greasy fries and a vanilla shake.

I know, a heart attack waiting to happen.

If there's any food group I choke on, it's those green vegetables. I just haven't found the flavor for broccoli, spinach, kale, or peas. I'll stomach a "thank you" helping if being a good guest requires it, provided I have a good glass of water to wash it down. I don't eat quiche, seafood, or anything more exotic than main street America.

Of course, my current eating habits were years in the making. When I was a kid, and I had the choice, the dessert bar was my hangout. I never thought about fat grams, calories, or portion sizes. As mentioned, I steered clear of anything green and even avoided surprisingly tasty foods such as steak (mostly due to the amount of extra chewing involved, I guess), sweet potatoes, and custard.

I'll admit that my food choices weren't without consequence.

One of the reasons many teenagers and young adults later walk away from the faith is because their spiritual food habits have led them into dysfunctional dining.

My once svelte and slim body now carries about fifty pounds more on its frame. I sometimes don't have the energy I once enjoyed and no longer participate in softball, basketball, and volleyball. I get winded just jumping to conclusions and jogging my memory.

That's why lately I've been thinking about eating better.

More balance. More healthy. More fiber. More fruits and vegetables.

It's the plan anyway. And it's all about choice.

It should also be the goal of every smaller-church children's ministry.

Small children don't eat a ton, so their food must be packed with nutrition. Little kids can be finicky too, so food must look good and taste great. In a smaller church, resources are limited and that's why every program has to be packed for maximum spiritual impact. Every program also needs to be carefully cooked—with respect to time, energy, and money—so it can effectively attract and assimilate children into a faith with Jesus.

CHILDREN'S SPIRITUAL NUTRITION

We tend to focus a lot of attention on children's nutritional needs. But kids also have spiritual needs too. Children need to be exposed to Christian fellowship, Bible study, service opportunities, worship experiences, and evangelistic moments. One of the reasons many teenagers and young adults later walk away from the faith is because their spiritual food habits have led them into dysfunctional dining, resulting in faith that's bulimic, obese, or anorexic. At the least, they've learned that Christianity isn't a main entrée for a full and healthy life, but rather an appetizer for moments of crisis, a soup for times of spiritual illness, and a dessert for Christmas or Easter.

We would do well to recognize that a child's needs differ greatly from an adult's. Children think differently. They respond to situations differently. They get involved differently. They make (and keep) friends differently. They worship differently. They learn differently. Children are active, and they delight in energetic games and boisterous noise. Our programs must intersect children at a variety of different need levels, whether cognitive, physical, mental, emotional, or spiritual. Children must not be viewed as underdeveloped, as inferior, as incapable, and, certainly not, as "mini-adults."

It's one of the primary "sins" I see all the time in children's ministry.

I affectionately call it "adult-ery," or the idea of forcing children into "adult" molds. Because an adult has different needs and lives within a different framework, it's tempting to force children into more mature frames for which they're not ready. We commit "adult-ery" (treat kids as adults) when we expect five-year-old Josh to spend an hour in a worship service without a squirm or a fidget, a whisper or a question. It's next to impossible for him. Adults may think that if children are sitting still, they are listening, but that assumption is "adult-erous."

Recently, I was on a flight with a precocious three-year-old first-time flyer. She was alive with comments, questions, and noises. She openly shared her fear of takeoff and landing. She sang aloud. And then there was the moment when a rather distinct foul smell wafted through the plane. She didn't hesitate to ask: "Mommy, who let a stinker?"

I had to smile at that one. But I watched other adults respond to this preschooler with varying emotions: disgust, chagrin, frustration, apathy, and amusement. Some "shhhh-ed" her. Some ignored her playful antics to get their attention. Still others shot disgusted looks at her mother who was trying to keep the girl occupied. Every adult had a frame that they were trying to fit this little girl into.

An effective children's minister will be knowledgeable of child developmental issues. In fact, it's key to preparing a well-balanced buffet of events, programs, activities, and learning opportunities to deepen a child's faith. Planning that buffet may challenge the smaller church, in particular, because the food service will be limited in offering due to size, money, volunteers, and time issues. The key is to create developmentally-designed programming that effectively reaches across the basic needs of a child.

A BALANCED BUFFET

Every children's ministry must offer a food drive that cooks up dynamic menus to attract children (based on their need) for a specific response, behavior, or attitude. Spiritual growth relies on a balanced diet of five key areas:

- Sweets and Treats (nonthreatening, high-caloric, fun activities that all children, regardless of their spiritual need, will enjoy)

- Appetizers (intentional attractive events and programs that introduce a child to a relationship with Jesus Christ)

- Soups and Breads (opportunities for children to use their talents and interests within a low-level commitment to the church)

- Vegetables (nutritious Christian education that serves to mature children in their faith and spiritual commitments)

- Meats (service projects that hone spiritual gifts, especially leadership skills, with a view towards ministry to other kids and adults)

**SW
CO**
Kid

I
wit
hu
mi
an
lik

SAMPLE "SWEETS"
bowling, hiking, camping, Wii video game tournaments, movies (G/PG), mall scavenger hunts, amusement parks, water parks, go-karts, video contests, game nights, karaoke, baseball games, zoos, kid-friendly museums, Christmas shopping, biking, skate days, 3-on-3 basketball tournaments, river floats (preteens only), Chuck E. Cheese's (or similar amusement) pizza parties, backyard pool parties, beach/lake days, roller skating, drive-in movies (at church), fishing, bonfire and s'mores, Halloween alternative (away from church), Fourth of July fireworks party (in a park), Super Bowl bash (in a home), fantasy sport leagues, mixers and community builders, parent/child nature walks, stuffed animal and real pet shows, picnics

These events, activities, and situations are nonthreatening, just-for-fun activities which children—whether churched or not—will find attractive and engaging. I'll be honest—many smaller churches miss the point of this level of programming because it seems so superficial.

But that's the point.

Some kids are still suckling milk. They're not ready for anything of substance. As mentioned in a previous chapter, in their worlds, they play video games, read Harry Potter books, watch *Hannah Montana*, and listen to bubblegum pop music. Essentially, they're seeking life experiences that make them feel good—about themselves, their friends, and their beliefs.

An effective children's minister will be knowledgeable of child developmental issues.

Some adults are tempted to sneak some veggies or hamburger into these sweet times, mostly because it's hard to create a purely entertainment event that doesn't have a "spiritual" or "biblical" focus. But yet, isn't any situation where "two are more are gathered" as Christians—whether it's a Bible study or a bike ride—a spiritual activity?

And if it draws even one child closer to a community of faith—even if not one word about Jesus is spoken—is that not scriptural ("He who is not with me is against me, and he who does not gather with me scatters [Matthew 12:30]")?

Smaller churches lean toward such thinking because they want to be thrifty with their use of volunteers and other resources. And because unchurched kids are there, it's natural for people to want to sprinkle on some Bible study. But that approach actually backfires and may even turn a kid off. When we use trickery and even deception (cloaking Christianity within a shell game that's "bait-and-switch") to persuade people toward a message, what are we saying about the message?

Children will feel tricked when they attend an event that advertises "fun and games" and are force-fed a devotional thought, a Bible object lesson, or even a time of worship. True "sweet and treat" events and activities are intentionally shallow, because that's where these kids live.

The goal is to connect kids into a faith community. No strings attached.

ASSORTED "APPETIZERS"

Vacation Bible School, church camp, Christian concerts, lock-ins, Halloween alternative (at church), Fourth of July fireworks party (at church), Super Bowl bash (at church), Upward basketball leagues, choirs, topical discussions, in-church pizza parties, parents' nights out, kids' musicals

APPETIZERS (GOAL: CONVERSION)

A secondary level of programming now invites "connected" kids to consider the next step in their faith: an authentic, personal decision to follow Jesus. These activities are slightly more nutritious and yet remain highly appetizing. They attract on two fronts: they're fun *and* friendly. In other words, these are events that kids talk about as highly enjoyable, but also will feature a large segment of their personal friends in attendance.

Kids like to hang with their friends.

"Appetizers" are attractive and always pull children toward the local church. They are also, essentially, evangelistic in nature. It's easy to take any of the "sweets and treats" activities and spiritually/biblically energize it into an "appetizer." Take a bike ride, with devotional studies at various sites on the trip. Enjoy a day at an amusement park that features a Christian concert (especially good for preteens). Show a movie with a strong Christian theme (e.g., "Facing the Giants") at the church.

The ultimate goal of appetizers is conversion. Children who experience these events should recognize that while these are fun activities, there is a clear message: Jesus is Lord and you need him.

In fact, if your event doesn't include some evangelistic moment to follow Jesus, then either you have short-changed the appetizer or your need to sweeten (remove any activities that are churchy) the event to be a fully nonthreatening situation for any child.

Every activity is spiritual, but each event can have a different target. You must be the one who decides which part of the buffet you are serving. If you aim right, you'll always hit the bull's-eye.

SOUPS AND BREADS (GOAL: COMMITMENT)

> **SUGGESTED "SOUPS AND BREADS"**
>
> Vacation Bible School, church camp, Christian concerts, lock-ins, worship bands, drama groups, puppet teams, interest clubs (photography, writing, art), children's church, book clubs, community builders with Bible discussions

Appetizers and sweets will attract kids, but their bite-sized content and low-nutritional (spiritual) value will hardly satisfy the greater spiritual needs of a child. This third level of programming seeks to meet a child's divine need for deeper friendships (accountability) and faith (spiritual gift use). Like appetizers, these activities and events are essentially nonthreatening (even to nonchurched children). But unlike appetizers and sweets, they are clearly designed to strengthen the faith of a child who has chosen to follow Jesus. They meet real needs and provide authentic answers to faith's doubts. These events show children that faith is a part of everyday life.

Just about any weekly children's meeting, other than Sunday school, qualifies as a soup and bread program. Ministry groups like children's choirs, puppet teams, worship bands, and drama groups are excellent examples. They're fun, they're a place where friends gather, and they provide exploration of faith.

VALUABLE "VEGGIES"
Sunday school, VBS, kids' sermons, children's worship experiences, backyard Bible studies, Bible "sword" drills, church camp, lock-ins/retreats (with spiritual themes and events), Christian music CD library

VEGETABLES (GOAL: CONVICTION)

In most cases, "vegetable" programming is the main entrée of a children's ministry, seeking to lead children to a deeper faith in God. Programs that challenge and inspire kids to a better walk with Jesus are considered the pick of the bunch. Sunday school. Vacation Bible School. Children's church. Retreats. Church camp. These programs do more than merely teach children about the faith, they also motivate and mature their Christianity. Such activities release children to find their roles within the church community.

Naturally, many smaller churches serve this course pretty well.

The smaller church has an advantage when it comes to this level of programming because it can personalize its offerings more easily than a larger church. Children have more opportunities to ask questions and leaders have far more flexibility in answering them. Teachers in small classes can tailor their curricula to the needs of every child who attends. One small church actually held a sixth-grade girls' class with only one member! That child received an inordinate and incredible Bible education from a devoted mentor and friend.

Children definitely need a heaping helping of prayer. At this level, kids are ready to participate in share-and-prayer opportunities. Again, smaller is actually better in the prayer department as children (and adults) are more likely to pray in a smaller group than a larger one. Furthermore, they'll also witness how their prayers are answered. Every child will have an opportunity to participate—no one gets lost in the crowd or shut down in the shuffle.

Invite children to actively participate in prayer moments. Encourage them to write or draw prayer requests on the church parking lot with colorful sidewalk chalk. Hold a prayer scavenger hunt where children seek out objects that best represent prayer needs in their lives. Use sensory experiences, such as prayer by candlelight or "tasteful" prayers (e.g., "Suck on a lemon drop and pray about a sour time in your life"). Pray quietly (no sound) or have children sing their prayers.

Vegetable programming is your opportunity to instruct children in the basics of the faith: what happened in the Bible and how we can respond to it. If presented creatively and experientially, these lessons will help children build a foundation for a lifetime.

The goal at this level is to convict and lead children to make positive and personal choices that reflect lives lived within the shadow of the cross.

"MEATS" (GOAL: COMMISSION)

The most intense and powerful element in children's ministry programming is when kids are released to use their abilities and gifts in service to God. A "meat" activity is the most difficult for children because it begins to mature them into leaders. It requires responsibility, dedication, and perseverance. But when we challenge and encourage children to master and express their gifts within service to others, we help them grow toward even more significant roles as they get older.

This level of programming is rarely done with smaller-church children's ministries. Partly, because it's a difficult level to get kids to approach, let alone operate. Many children are skeptical of adults who want them to "serve," as the "service" tends to be for an adult's ego, agenda, or selfishness. Yet, once again, a smaller church has a distinct advantage. Smaller congregations are eagerly seeking someone—anyone—to serve.

> ### MARVELOUS "MEATS"
>
> create artwork for senior citizens, go Christmas caroling, conduct nursing-home services, participate in an adopt-a-grandparent program, deliver flowers to shut-ins, bake cookies and make cards for ill children, clean the church building, sing or play special music for adult worship, read Scripture for church, serve as ushers, organize a toy drive, collect presents for prisoners, serve in the nursery (older children), lead in children's church, supply a devotional or testimony in worship, write praise songs, create newsletters, build a Web page, e-mail visitors or absent children, collect food for local shelter, organize Bible drives

Meat activities encourage children to reach out into their neighborhoods, their schools, their churches, and their communities to be "missionaries." Children at this level rarely need a kudo or compliment. What they want is for an adult to truly notice. Once they catch the vision of what they can do for God, it'll be hard to shut them down.

Meat programming doesn't have to be complicated. Children learn from small projects as well as larger service opportunities. Sometimes meat activities involve children in small tasks, such as washing dishes, sweeping the fellowship hall, or carrying out the trash. Again, the smaller church has an advantage because in a less-populated community there is always room for a job. You might involve your fifth graders in big projects, such as leading backyard Bible studies for younger children. Through big and small events, children learn that even they can contribute to God's work.

In most settings, older children will be best prepared for meat programs, though younger children can still be involved in limited ways. Preschoolers are too young for most service projects, but they can help make no-bake cookies for the pastor or share hugs with senior church members. Middle-graders are ready participants because they are eager to please others. And preteens can even lead some activities without adult supervision.

A balanced smaller-church children's program will feature service-oriented op-portunities for kids. The goal at this final level is to commission children to make a difference in their world and to serve as Jesus served. Children at any level can serve through their gifts, no matter their spiritual maturity.

PASS ANOTHER HELPING PLEASE . . .

Some might say it's impossible for a smaller church to provide programming in all five of these areas. However, with proper balance and sensible portion sizes (watch the temptation to overprogram), you'll find that it's truly possible. We don't need to provide all of these levels on an ongoing basis. In fact, depending on your group, you may not need to offer meats yet. It's too chewy and the spiri-tual teeth are still forming.

On the other hand, if you provide only vegetables and meats, you'll discover your children's ministry has stalled. The sweets and appetizers may not hold much nutritional value, but they do possess the key to growing a children's ministry.

The key is to let the children serve as the measuring stick. If the children in your church are growing and excited about God, then your ministry is successful even if your calendar doesn't list a single children's ministry activity for every level of programming. You may find that once you have several children involved in vegetable meetings (e.g., Sunday school, children's church, VBS), you can go light on the appetizers for a few months.

Finally, almost every idea in this chapter can be adapted, altered, or arranged in a manner suitable to even the smallest children's group. Tailor your buffet of events to the needs of the kids. Add and subtract programs as necessary. The goal is a balanced diet of activities and programs that are engaging, enjoyable, and enlightening.

Now, I don't know about you, but all this food-talk has made me hungry.

Time for a burger, hold the mayo, and easy on the fries!

CHAPTER 6

Volunteer On!

> "'Come, follow me,' Jesus said, 'and I will make you fishers of men.'"
>
> (MATTHEW 4:19)

've never been much of a fisherman. The patience, persistence, and practice of fishing have never appealed to me. Hot, sweaty, and sunburned. Cold, numb, and frostbitten. Stinky, long hours, exhausted for little return. The frustrations of snags, lost tackle, or a nagging spouse (who can't understand your passion for trolling, bait shops, and rods) only adds to the woes.

No, for me fishing is a pastime that I entertain only occasionally.

But for my brother, he lives to fish. Randy is a master angler who could have a PhD in ichthyology. He purposely moved near Portland, Oregon, to fish even more. He has a specially designed boat that's able to get him into the ocean waters. He owns countless lures, poles, and gadgets (like a GPS fish finder) to improve his chances of catching the lunker. Randy knows the waters and the fish he seeks, and he is willing to sacrifice to make it happen.

Recently I was in Portland, and Randy invited me on a fishing expedition. The coho salmon were running and the weather was perfect for "crossing the bar" into the Pacific. I quickly learned the cost to cast isn't cheap. Fishing license. Motion sickness medication. And a 3 AM departure (in order to make high tide).

Despite a short night and a long ride to Astoria, the Columbia River soon washed away any reservations. I realized this was something special. On board was a former commercial fisherman who probably forgot more about these waters than I'll ever know. After sailing nine miles past the mouth of the Columbia into the open Pacific, we finally dropped our lines baited with fresh herring.

When trolling for volunteers, it takes patience, persistence, and right practices.

"Fish on!" someone yelled immediately. The pole was bending in a wild dance as I jumped to reel in the prize. The ten-pound coho fought hard, but I won the war.

Within two hours, we had caught our limit and had thrown back several more. At times, we couldn't bait more than one line because as soon as it hit the water, another silver salmon was hooked.

Which made me wonder.

Wouldn't it be nice to have the same luck finding volunteers?

The primary frustrations of most churches, but especially smaller ones, focus upon finding, training, retaining, and motivating volunteers. Finding the right ones can be tough. Those who are willing aren't always skilled. And it seems as though those who would really shine in ministry often say no.

The phrase most discouraging to those in children's ministry may be "Get someone else."

When trolling for volunteers, it takes patience, persistence, and right practices. There's also a cost to catching a volunteer and keeping him or her on line. Getting someone to initially "hit" on your program need is the easy part; keeping that person hooked is something different. The good news is that you can learn what lures volunteers and respond appropriately to reel in individuals you never imagined were possible catches.

FEED THE NEED

The secret to fishing is the bait. An empty hook does nothing. It's also important to know the fish and what they crave. You don't use worms with walleyes and perch don't go for plugs. Nevertheless, every living thing has a need to ingest and digest. For humans, our stomachs growl when we're hungry. Inner hungers will drive a person to extreme solutions, extraordinary opportunities, and exhilarating experiences.

What are those inner needs? What drives someone to bite? Just think about the G-R-O-W-L-S. Grace. Relationships. Ownership. Worth. Laughter. Safety/Security. I will guarantee if you feed these inner hungers, you'll do very little recruiting. In fact, you'll have people jumping into your ministry boat!

• **The first need is for *grace*.** This is the divine need that's often missed by secular psychologists, such as Abraham Maslow and William Glasser (who have created similar hierarchies of human needs). Grace is unconditional, amazing, wild, extreme, and wholly unfair. Grace recognizes justice should be served, but covers it with forgiveness. Grace allows for mistakes, mishaps, and messes.

Volunteers hunger to work in an environment where grace abounds. Does that mean there are no consequences? Certainly not. But a natural consequence

RESOURCES SPOTLIGHT

Care & Feeding of Volunteers by Barbara Bolton, et. al. (Standard Publishing). This excellent resource gives 12 user-friendly training sessions to manage and motivate your volunteers. Perfect for smaller churches!

Take-out Training for Teachers and *Teacher Training on the Go* by Keith Johnson (Group Publishing). Discover simple solutions for training teachers within their busy lifestyles. Both books feature reproducible handouts and CDs with inspirational insights and teaching tips.

is different than an executed punishment. For example, my volunteer staff is expected to attend one training event every year (at my expense) or they cannot serve. But my "grace" is offering four to five training opportunities so busy calendars can freely adjust.

• **A second inner need is a desire for *relationships*.** Humans are relational beings. We love to connect, converse, and collect shared experiences. Too many volunteers feel like lone rangers trapped on an island: nowhere to ride and no Tonto in sight. A relational volunteer ministry will regularly join the team together for sharing, prayer, training, news, and policies. A monthly e-newsletter to all volunteers can serve this purpose. Or a monthly (brief) staff meeting. Or an annual all-expense paid volunteer retreat. Regular correspondence (affirmations, instructions) and recognition (birthdays, anniversaries) also reveal connection.

Smaller churches might feel these relational moments will backfire (who has the time?), but if these meetings, retreats, and correspondence create connection, volunteers will positively respond. In my experience with children's and youth ministries, most volunteers quit not because they don't like the work but because they feel they're doing it alone.

• ***Ownership* is a third need.** Every individual wants to contribute and have a sense of power. I have a photo of a youth meeting I led during my college years. The kids are having fun. I'm having a ball. It's a great picture! Until you look closely and notice the volunteer staff, lined up against the wall with arms folded. It's no wonder shortly after that photo was snapped I lost half my team. I thought they didn't feel called, but the photo reveals they didn't have ownership.

A common misperception is that ownership is doing assigned work, but that's not true. Ownership allows a volunteer to be released within his own power, talent, and desires to *create* work. If I (as the leader) tell a volunteer to bring games for the next children's event, that's assigned work. But if I share a need for someone to bring a game or allow a volunteer to suggest "games would be great" for this event, I create an option and choice for involvement. Too many smaller churches get their work done via "assignments." Instead, step back and let your volunteers choose their parts to sing. You'll soon hear a far different tune.

• **A fourth inner need is *worth*.** It's not enough to merely have contribution and control (power), but also recognition. Think of it this way: every volunteer has a value gas tank that requires continual refueling and topping off. When a worker drives on fumes alone, he'll become a casualty. Everyone yearns to be noticed, featured, awarded, valued, recognized, acknowledged, thanked, appreciated, and respected. It's what keeps us going when nothing else is working.

Ownership allows a volunteer to be released within his own power, talent, and desires to create work.

A smaller-church children's ministry can easily create an environment where workers feel valued. Volunteer spotlights. Volunteer appreciation months. My language of love is gifts and so I enjoy giving volunteers tokens of my appreciation. The key is to listen to what they like and to hopefully include yourself in the moment (to key in on the relationship need). For example, a male volunteer who enjoys baseball would feel valued if I purchased two tickets (one for him and one for me) to a game. A female volunteer who has young children underfoot would freely welcome a gift certificate and a night of complimentary babysitting. It means you hear their angst and respect their desires.

One caveat: any gifting is a matter of grace, not reward. It's freely given and always from within a relational perspective ("I know you would like this pleasure"). It also avoids competition. When we award a team member, there should be celebratory applause and not divisive disapproval ("Why didn't I get that accolade?"). Awarding is natural and consequential. Rewarding taps into human greed and makes the prize more important than the job. Personally, I prefer to award in private and appreciate in public. That is, I will recognize a team member's contributions publicly, but will privately and personally share a treat for a job well done.

• ***Laughter* is a fifth need of volunteers.** Girls just want to have fun, but boys do too! Think about something you love doing. Something you'd spend money to enjoy. Something that makes you relax and have a good time. I bet you're smiling just thinking about it. Exactly. When we smile and laugh, we tap into an inner need. I don't understand marathon runners, golfers, or soccer players. I get no special enjoyment from even watching them, but I have friends who smile as they run, drive, and kick the ball.

A smaller-church children's ministry will attract more volunteers if it concentrates on creating a fun ministry. And let's face it: working with children is fun! They're cute. They say strange things (especially preteens). And they like to laugh. What cripples a children's ministry is when we focus on the frowns. An effective leader will make working with kids a hoot. He will design a learning environment that's enjoyable for both teacher and student. She will create programs (like VBS) that feature so much fun you must volunteer again (and again and again).

• **The final need is for *safety/security*.** Every person must feel safe—emotionally, physically, mentally, and spiritually. Leaders must carefully construct sanctuaries and safe zones. The last place a person should be hurt is at church. In fact, a safe program will attract the hurting. As you consider the need for safety and security, think about these four areas of safety:

What cripples a children's ministry is when we focus on the frowns.

Physical Safety. How safe are your classrooms? When was the last time you in-spected space, toys, and activities for dangers? Is your nursery sanitized and deodor-ized? Do you feed children healthy snacks on Sunday mornings? Do you feed them at all (many come to church hungry)? Do you allow fighting, biting, hitting, and other physical abuse? Do your volunteers feel physically safe?

Emotional Safety. Are your classes, activities, and events free of negative emo-tions (anger, apathy, anxiety) by both volunteers and participants? Are your teachers trained to help kids unpack the emotional baggage they bring to class or church?

Mental Safety. Can a volunteer freely ask any question without fear of embarrass-ment or punishment? Are volunteers encouraged to be learners? Is your children's ministry a place rich in learning opportunity?

Spiritual Safety. Do volunteers feel safe to express their spirituality, even if it's different from yours? Is doctrinal conformity a value or vice grip to which volunteers must bow? Are volunteers given encouragement and opportunities for spiritual growth? How well do you know the backgrounds, journeys, and present conditions of your volunteers' spirituality?

Ultimately, if you dedicate your energies to baiting and feeding the needs of volunteers, you will not only recruit a better volunteer but you'll also do it less often (because satisfied volunteers stay put).

BAITING THE HOOK (RECRUITING)

Recruiting is not a seasonal sport. It doesn't happen a month before the start of the next Sunday school year. The search for the next solid volunteer is always happening. So how do you find great volunteers?

> **RESOURCES ▲ SPOTLIGHT**
>
> **Background Checks!**
>
> It's important to screen every volunteer prior to releasing them to work with children. Not every background check is the same, however, so do your research before landing on a protective agency. Recommended links include:
>
> www.protectmyministry.com
>
> www.churchstaffing.com
>
> www.volunteerselectplus.com
>
> www.3dchurchcheck.com
>
> You can also check with your church's insurance company for specifics on what criteria to follow in background checks. Often insurance companies will provide information, as well as specific forms they require to be used.

• **Look for volunteers of all occupations.** No volunteer is the same. Some have been trained; many have not. Some enjoy working personally with children, while others welcome a more indirect opportunity (like driving the van). A few can organize, while others support. Occupation makes no difference (CEO, janitor, professor, or plumber). Age doesn't matter either. In fact, some of the best children's workers are teenagers and older adults.

Is there a volunteer to avoid? Absolutely. Children's ministry isn't the place for adults seeking to recapture their childhood. Nor is it only a chaperone situation. Children's ministry needs workers, not watchers. It's also not the job for those who seek to be moral advisors. Kids need adult mentors, not messages. They need a hand to hold, not a cliché to memorize. Look for volunteers in whom you can *see* Jesus. If you can't see him, neither will the kids.

• **Evaluate personal interests and gifts.** As you recruit, match people to positions. Organized adults can easily plan day trips, develop curriculum, or design events. Adults who enjoy writing will welcome opportunities to edit and publish newsletters or type correspondence. Drama enthusiasts will jump to lead puppet ministries, dramas for children's church, or clown ministry. Musical adults love to lead worship or a children's choir.

Sometimes you need photographers, cooks, drivers, painters, publicists, seam-stresses, Web masters, carpenters, fundraisers, missionaries, and teachers. Rather than recruit a few to wear many hats, recruit several people—with various gifts and interests—to wear a few hats each. It's easier to enlist someone for a fifteen-minute task than a fifteen-hour (or fifteen-month) tour of duty.

• **Create success early.** When we toss volunteers into situations beyond their abilities, they'll easily become discouraged. And they'll likely say no when asked to renew their commitments.

Conversely, volunteers who experience positive ministry moments not only enjoy their work but also find personal purpose in it. Start new volunteers with small, fun projects. Allow them to experience a minor success, such as going along on a zoo trip; then begin to challenge them with more commanding roles.

Schedule a training time for new teachers before they begin teaching; then have new teachers work with more experienced teachers until they get their legs. Observe the instruction of new teachers and encourage mature teachers to serve as mentors. The more comfortable a new teacher feels, the more success she'll experience.

One more thing: keep asking! Ask openly. Ask widely. Ask regularly.

I am amazed how many times I heard rumors that the children's coordinator at my church couldn't find help. In fact, had I been aware of a volunteer need, I would have willingly helped. I was just unaware. So don't assume anything.

WHEN VOLUNTEERS DON'T BITE

A children's ministry coordinator can easily be discouraged by the explanations people offer for not volunteering. Here are five of these reasons and some solid solutions to their objections.

• **"I'd rather work with teenagers or adults."** For some adults, working with children is considered a waste of their talents. It lacks glamour. After all, preteen craft projects and nursery duty hardly seem as striking as youth mission trips to Mexico.

The problem is that many churches rarely expose their children's ministry to the whole congregation. Consequently, it's easy to think that to volunteer for children's ministry means exile to a dark basement with only Kool-Aid and stale cookies for refreshments.

The issue is *perception*. How is your children's ministry perceived by other adults? Get the children (and volunteers) out front. Create opportunities for them to shine from the stage. Coordinate a quarterly children's Sunday. Make service in children's ministry a privilege, not a prison sentence. Encourage volunteers to share testimonies by video or publicly. Help adults realize how impressionable children are and how their lives can change a kid forever. Life on life influence is attractive to many adults seeking purpose.

Another idea is to encourage current volunteers to recruit new helpers. People who enjoy what they're doing will naturally recruit through their enthusiasm. A motivated volunteer staff will draw notice from other adults.

You can also encourage skeptical volunteers to part-time or one-time service. Generally, just being around children is fun and inviting, and skepticism will dissolve as the volunteer becomes involved.

• **"I don't want to do what people did to me."** Some potential volunteers recall the emotional bumps and bruises of their own religious training, especially by adults who led them, and they fear they'll inflict the same atrocities on the next generation.

Naturally, you can't fault people for this feeling and, in fact, it's best to meet it head on. One possible strategy is to encourage such individuals to serve as assistant teachers or leaders. Work them into the program slowly by asking them to serve as greeters, attendance-takers, supply assistants, or readers. Let them observe the ways that other teachers interact with children and to witness positive examples of good church relationships. Hopefully, they'll realize what they experienced was not normal, nor how they will respond.

Another option is to introduce skeptical volunteers to kids through nonthreatening "dessert" and "appetizer" events (see Chapter 5). Adults love to tag along on fun activities and often find the children really like them (and need them). Using a newer volunteer for this type of event can provide personal insight into what type of volunteer the person is and how you can best use the individual in your ministry.

• **"My child is (or isn't) in the group."** Parents make excellent volunteers. I find husband-and-wife teams to be particularly positive. Children need good family role models and couples that serve as leaders/teachers are almost always successful. Spouses also hold one another accountable, provide extra creativity, and split responsibilities.

Some parents want to serve but prefer to avoid direct interaction with their own children. They want their kids to have other adult role models. Such parents can easily be involved as support staff or as volunteers for a different age group.

On the other hand, some parents won't serve unless they're with their children. Don't view this as necessarily being overprotective. Some parents and their children enjoy learning and being together. Church is one of the few places where they can enjoy that benefit.

Nevertheless, you will have overprotective types, including a few who distrust anyone but *them* with their kids. If the children are older, seek the kids' input (do they want Mom or Dad around?). Deal with the parents gently and encourage them to allow their children to grow on their own. And remember, leaders have the final say. An overprotective parent cannot be a volunteer unless you allow it. Parents may remove their children, but that consequence may be far less damaging than what can happen if they serve.

The majority of parents make wonderful volunteers. Be cautious, however: parenthood doesn't automatically qualify a person to be a teacher or leader. We must not look down on any who avoids working with children because he or she sincerely doesn't feel qualified. Not everyone has the personality, creativity, energy, or patience to teach children, and some parents accurately recognize their limitations. Parents also need a break from their kids and those who choose not to help shouldn't be led to feel guilty. Rather, affirm and encourage their involvement whenever they are able.

• **"I'm scared!"** Fear can cause many volunteers to resist children's ministry. Sometimes they fear failure or rejection or even simple tasks like public speaking.

Good training can melt many fears. Too often smaller churches throw frightened, untrained recruits into classrooms. This leads to disaster and discouragement. Teachers who aren't adequately trained will often quit because they feel as though they're doing a bad job (remember the inner need to feel "worth").

RESOURCES SPOTLIGHT

Volunteer Helps

Many curriculum publishers provide helps for recruiting, training, and retaining volunteers. Using the keyword "volunteers," check out the helps available from the following:

www.standardpub.com

www.group.com

www.gospellight.com

Quarterly (and sometimes monthly) training is common in churches—especially smaller ones—that successfully recruit and retain workers. Training doesn't have to be lengthy or complicated. You can train in just 10 seconds (using the ideas given on pages 99 or 104)! And you can make training fun by incorporating team-building activities and moments for recognitions (using the extended ideas on pages 100–103 or 105–108).

On-the-job training enables new recruits to develop their own abilities. Team-teaching is an excellent strategy to help hesitant teachers become more involved. Unfortunately, few smaller churches use team-teaching. "It's hard enough to find one teacher," a weary coordinator once shared. "How will I find two?" But you can take this one to the bank: the reason many don't volunteer is they fear they'll go it *alone.* Team-teaching removes that fear and, consequently, more will volunteer for the work.

• **"I'll be here forever!"** Many smaller churches are proud of their abilities to retain teachers for years and years (and years). It's certainly a goal worth pursuing. Unfortunately, some teachers keep serving out of guilt. I've known some leaders to badger teachers to remain, despite their need for a real break. A guilty volunteer will soon grow resentful and also less effective. In fact, shaming volunteers into "until death do us part" service sends a clear and dangerous message to potential workers: if you get in, you stay in . . . for life!

Personally, I prefer one-year contractual agreements for teachers and leaders. In fact, these agreements actually diffuse many of the bombs waiting to blow in children's ministry. A teacher contract outlines expectations, duties, and standards of conduct. It will often require training as well. I've also found that a nine-month agreement is best, leaving summer free for volunteers to relax and recharge (see the guidelines for creating a Teacher Contract on page 109).

VOLUNTEER ON!

Fishermen love to tell stories and share their adventures.

So do volunteers.

A children's ministry that creates an environment of grace, relationships, ownership, worth, laughter, and safety/security for its workers will succeed.

When the fishing is real good, it's impossible to do anything else but bait, reel, and net. These situations don't come by accident, but by intentional design.

Volunteers won't just jump into your boat either. In fact, they won't even crawl onto land. You have to know what your volunteers enjoy, what baits them, what drives them, and what keeps them coming back for more.

Grace releases workers to make mistakes and lose the fear of failure.

Relationships bond a team and reduce feelings of isolation.

Ownership empowers volunteers to have contribution and control.

Worth fuels workers with a sense of purpose and value.

Laughter explodes boredom, apathy, and negativism.

Safety and *Security* creates comfort and peace.

Feed these needs and you'll always have workers waiting.

Volunteer on!

Better Safe Than Sued

Team-teaching can help avoid many potential problems. Many churches now employ the "two adult" rule to lead every class or activity where children are involved. This standard minimizes opportunities for misconduct by individuals, and it protects your volunteers from false accusations. The accountability also makes parents more comfortable.

Few smaller churches typically screen volunteers who work with children. Even fewer will require background checks. Nevertheless you should screen all volunteers. Child molesters often find easy access into churches, especially smaller congregations that desperately need help.

Here are a few additional screening tips:

Use a detailed application form. Get a written statement from the applicant that he or she has no background of impropriety with children.

Interview volunteers. Develop a qualified team to interview potential workers. Local police or social service agencies can offer training or advice. Ask probing interview questions: "Why are you interested in children's work?" "Have you ever been accused of impropriety?"

Check for criminal activities. Explain to applicants your purpose in using background checks. Get a written release from the potential volunteer and complete a criminal records check. If an applicant refuses to cooperate, don't permit that person to work with children. The only people who dislike background checks are those with something to hide. Even if you feel you know the person well, it's still best to screen.

Contact references. Request references from individuals who've known the applicant in other settings (personal, educational, and professional), even if the person is (again) well known to your ministry.

Require a waiting period. Wait at least six months before moving new applicants into ministry. Few true molesters will wait that long when they can have quicker access at another church.

Many smaller churches will consider these suggestions as unrealistic. Perhaps so. But unfortunately those who fail to adequately screen their volunteers expose themselves to potential heartache and lawsuits.

Training 1: "Creative Teaching"

10-Second Training
(for instant training moments)

Statement: "Drive for show, putt for dough."

Meaning: Creativity is vital, but intentional teaching causes learning.

1-Minute Training
(for hallway conversations with teachers)

"Drive for show, putt for dough." It's a common cliché in golf, but a world of wisdom in teaching. The art of teaching is creativity. It's the impressive activities that prompt "oohs" and "ahs" from the learners. But an incredible activity—like a long drive in golf—is meaningless if it takes countless additional putts to score the hole. Creativity in the classroom is equally impressive but tragically empty unless the teacher can cause learning to occur.

Question: **What type of grade would you give your creativity quotient in the classroom?**

10-Minute Training
(a 10-minute teacher-training meeting)

Drop a golf ball and take a putt in front of the teachers. Say: **In the world of golf, there's a saying: "Drive for show, putt for dough."** Pause and then ask the teachers to share what they believe the cliché means.

After some responses, say: **Teaching is a lot like golf. The drive in our lessons is the creative activities we do to maintain interest and change pace. However, these creative learning activities mean little if we, as teachers, cannot communicate the truth in the end. On the other hand, you can have a good handle on truth to be taught, but lose the hole because you can inspire and attract learner interest. Master teachers, like golfers, know you don't drive with a putter or putt with a driver. However, if you can balance creativity with communication, everyone wins.**

Form trios or quads and discuss:

• Why is it so hard to be creative as a teacher? What are the barriers?

• Can a teacher be too creative? Why or why not?

• Can a teacher concentrate so much on communicating the truth (getting the ball in the hole) that she causes apathy and boredom? Explain.

After three to four minutes, discuss your conclusions and share ideas.

Encourage the teachers to brainstorm strategies for being creative. After a couple more minutes, share strategies and commit to more creative excellence.

1-Hour Training
(a 1-hour teacher-training session)

Before the meeting, create a golf pro putting area. Lay down green Astro-Turf® carpet and, if available, lay out a putting green. You'll need some putters and golf balls. Paper cups on their sides can serve as holes, if needed.

To start the meeting, have each teacher take a round and record how many shots are taken to put the ball in the cup. After all teachers have all taken their turn, stop and welcome them to the training meeting and say, **Drive for show, putt for dough.** Then ask:

• What do you think this cliché, from the world of golf, means?

• How is "driving for show" like the use of creativity in a classroom?

• How is "putting for dough" like effective communication that results in learning in a classroom?

Say, **Creative communication is both an art and science. The art of teaching is creative learning activities that we incorporate to keep learner's interest and invoke thought. The science of teaching is actually scoring the putt. In the end, we have to get it in the hole. In learning, that means that a student must learn or we haven't truly taught.**

Instruct teachers to create trios or quads and answer these questions:

• Why is it so hard to be creative as a teacher?

• Can a teacher be too creative? Why or why not?

• Can a teacher concentrate so much on communicating the truth (getting the ball in the hole) that she causes apathy and boredom? Explain.

Show a clip from the movie, *Miracle on 34th Street*, where Santa Claus is explaining to the little girl that there are all sorts of *nations* in the world, but the greatest is the *imagination*. After the clip, ask: **What are the barriers to creativity in the classroom? How can we be more imaginative, as teachers?** (This discussion can give you insight into what your teachers might need in resources to better their teaching experiences.)

Invite teachers to choose from one of three different groups: writing, drama, or music. If there are more than four people in an interest area, form subgroups of four or five. Each group needs to brainstorm how a teacher can be more creative and then complete its assignment:

• Writing Group: Create a parody of "The Night Before Christmas" that outlines Santa not coming to visit a home, but creativity arriving to help a teacher teach. To get started: "Twas the night before the lesson and all through the teacher's mind . . ."

• Drama Group: Create a commercial for a new product known as "Creativity Enhancement" pills.

• Music Group: Revise the lyrics to "RESPECT" (by Aretha Franklin) to "C-R-E-A-T-E" and develop a parody that reveals the reasons why teachers should be creative in the classroom.

Allow the groups ten to twelve minutes to create their productions and then have each group present its parody. Encourage wild applause after each presentation.

Say: **Isn't it fun to be creative? I think one of the reasons we don't try to be more creative is that we're afraid. What if our idea is strange? or doesn't work? Did you know that Thomas Edison failed over and over again? And yet, his creative inventions changed the face of our world. He was willing to "drive for show" even when he was booed or laughed at. Of course, when he hit the hole and made a difference, the world clapped.**

Give each teacher a golf ball and permanent marker. Encourage each person to write on the ball one strategy or idea for being more creative in the classroom and draw a picture of himself teaching in the classroom. After a couple minutes, invite each teacher to take one more putt with his or her ball. As teachers putt, they can share with the rest of the group their "creativity commitments." Close in prayer.

Training 2: "Motivating Children"

10-Second Training
(for instant training moments)

Statement: "Feed the need, not the greed."

Meaning: Prizes and gimmicks will persuade for the moment, but only feeding inner needs truly last.

1-Minute Training
(for hallway conversations with teachers)

"Feed the need, not the greed." It's tempting to use external motivation (prizes, rewards, food, treats) to encourage children to behave, learn, and respond. The problem is these gimmicks only "massage the message"; they do not touch the true inner needs of a child. Master teachers feed the inner G-R-O-W-L-S of a child: grace, relationships, ownership, worth, laughter, and safety and security.

Question: **How do you motivate children to behave and belong?**

10-Minute Training

(a 10-minute teacher-training meeting)

Supplies: 5 large Snickers® bars, 2 bags of Snickers® miniatures

Say: **We're going to start with a fairly common game in children's ministry! I need five volunteers to come forward.** Encourage, coax, and share that the winners will receive a nice big candy bar for completing the task. Try to secure at least three participants.

When you have the volunteers, share that each one will have one chance to quote Ephesians 2:8, 9 from memory and with no mistakes. Allow the volunteers thirty seconds to review a PowerPoint slide of the verse and then test each one.

The remaining volunteers serve as judges and whenever a mistake is made, they must form an L on their foreheads and say loudly "LOSER!" This will be very uncomfortable for some volunteers, but that's okay. It's part of this learning experience.

Give each recruited volunteer one chance to quote Ephesians 2:8, 9. If someone manages (few will!) to quote it without a mistake, give him a large Snickers bar.

Form groups, with one of the game volunteers in each one group. Ask groups to discuss the following questions.

• How did it feel to be the one quoting the verses? a judge? Which was a more difficult task? Why?

• How is this experience like (or unlike) how we motivate children to say memory verses, bring their Bibles, invite friends, or even behave?

• What did you learn from this experience for the next time you teach?

After three to four minutes, discuss your conclusions and share ideas. Encourage the teachers to brainstorm strategies for motivating children without gimmicks, bribery, treats, treasures, or Bible Bucks. Remind teachers of the message of Ephesians 2:8, 9: We are saved by grace, not works.

End the session by showering everyone with Snickers miniatures!

1-Hour Training

(a 1-hour teacher-training session)

Start the meeting with the experiential exercise developed in the "10-Minute Training" session. After showering the volunteers with Snickers miniatures, say: **It's important to watch how we motivate children. Certainly the easiest path may not be the best. External motivation is rooted in behavioral psychology (originating in the early 20th century) that essentially believed that man was nothing more than an evolved animal that could be trained like a dog to behave and even learn. The problem is we aren't dogs! And every human being hungers for something deeper. When you're hungry, your stomach growls. Similarly, we all have six inner needs that we want fed and they spell "G-R-O-W-L-S": Grace, Relationships, Ownership, Worth, Laughter, and Safety/Security.**

Instruct teachers to create trios or quads. Then lead them through each "need" with a brief description and explanation. (Feel free to use personal examples and illustrations.)

GRACE: the hunger for unconditional acceptance and love
RELATIONSHIPS: the hunger for authentic connection and companionship
OWNERSHIP: the hunger to contribute and control (power)
WORTH: the hunger to feel valued
LAUGHTER: the hunger to find pleasure and enjoyment
SAFETY/SECURITY: the hunger to satisfy basic physical, emotional, mental, and spiritual needs

After each need, instruct the groups to answer these questions (allow five minutes for each need):

• What is it about this particular need that truly motivates us?

• How does the use of external motivators (prizes, treats, etc.) actually short-circuit this particular need?

• What is one strategy you could employ to "feed this need" in your work with children?

Encourage volunteers to memorize the G-R-O-W-L-S acronym and to continually seek ways to create learning environments where children feel grace and have rich relational experiences that invite opportunities for them to contribute, have a sense of personal worth, laugh, and feel secure and safe.

As a whole group, discuss the consequences of using external motivators such as Bible Bucks, candy, and prizes as motivational methods. Be aware who you may have some (perhaps even you, as the leader) that disagree with the idea that all such gimmicks are in poor taste. That's okay. This is a time to explore various motivational techniques. Be cautious is sharing your view, at first, and encourage the volunteers to discuss the consequences (pros and cons) for using rewards in children's ministry. Some might note that "rewards" are biblical, but the use of "reward" in Scripture is far different than how it's used in today's classroom. You'd be hard-pressed to find Jesus, or any other biblical leader, motivating his followers with treats or treasures. Jesus met natural needs (feeding the 5,000). He didn't bait his disciples with incentives for getting the answer right.

After an extended time of discussion, say: **It's very important to properly motivate a child. The methods we use to win a kid are what we'll probably need to keep him. Frankly, a safe and secure children's ministry that is fueled by grace, positive relationships, ownership, worth, and laughter will be attractive—both for the kids and the adults who serve them.**

End in prayer, seeking special wisdom from God to properly motivate the children.

Teacher Contract

A teacher's contract is best created by the volunteers themselves. At your next teacher's meeting, spend about thirty minutes brainstorming the teaching standards that *every* teacher in your church should adhere to in order to remain a teacher in the program. Consider these questions:

What controls should be created to make sure teachers adhere to these standards?

What should we expect in the following areas from every teacher?

• Church membership/attendance

• Spiritual life of the teacher

• The role of the teacher's family

• Basic teaching skills

• Availability for meetings

• Knowledge of Scripture, theology, etc.

• Teachability and willingness to be trained

• Weekly responsibilities/tasks

• Responsibility to teaching team and church

Key Components

What will you, the teacher, do for the church?

What will we, the church, do to help you teach and lead?

Brainstorm any resources the church should provide for the volunteer. Create a working document that, in time, can actually become a "Teacher's Covenant." The key is to let the volunteers set the standards and not you, the leader.

CHAPTER 7

Money Matters

> *"I know what it is to be in need, and I know what it is to have plenty.*
>
> *I have learned the secret of being content in any and every situation, whether well fed or hungry, whether living in plenty or in want. I can do everything through him who gives me strength."*
>
> (PHILIPPIANS 4:12, 13)

Money matters. From Wall Street to Main Street, the cash box calculates who's in and who's out, who's hot and who's not, who's got it and who doesn't. On TV, the show *Mad Money* is popular. Coach Cramer lays out on Friday all the plays needed to make money when the bell rings on Monday. Lotteries, casinos, and millionaire shows promise quick bucks and overnight lifestyles of the rich and now famous.

In a consumer culture, American churches can easily be swindled into thinking that a solution to every problem is just an offering plate away. But just like real life economics, the real truth is that pennies wisely saved lend themselves to richer rewards and blessings.

Financial issues trouble churches of all sizes, but the smaller church tends to be the hardest hit. For most, second to finding volunteers is the frustration of money (or the lack thereof).

When funds are tight or limited or frozen, it's tough to decide what is necessity and what is a frivolous expense. Some smaller churches have learned to discern what they really need and to plan for it, but many others bounce between extravagance and penny-pinching frugality. In fact, one noticeable change in the past fifteen years has been how "boomer" elderships have released the financial floodgates, much to the disdain of "depression-era" leaders who saved every penny for a rainy day. Consequently, many smaller churches have overspent or nonchalantly drained the coffers on part-time youth ministers, projection units, computers, and electronic media. Ultimately they have discovered that money can't buy church growth.

Sometimes the wisest financial choice a smaller church can make is to discontinue an expensive, ineffective program (no matter how long the tradition).

To boost success, smaller churches must continually ask, "Is what we're doing the best thing to do? Would other strategies be better or more cost effective?"

Let me illustrate. As a youth ministry professor, I have helped match many churches with my graduating seniors. While purely anecdotal, the average annual salary of a full-time youth minister, fresh from college, is between $25 to $30 thousand a year. Furthermore, the average youth minister will stay in a smaller congregation less than three years (most leave within two years!). It will cost another five grand to seek, secure, and move another youth minister. That's $75,000 dollars invested in an inexperienced youth minister who mostly likely won't see the freshmen graduate high school. By the way, the graduates with experience command as much as $10 grand more and tend to land medium to large churches the day after they grab the sheepskin.

Still think a youth minister is a good investment?

What if your church sunk $25,000 every year into your present youth program for the training of volunteers, resources, curricula, and upgraded equipment? What if you invested this would-be salary into scholarships for children to attend camps, conferences, and even (down the road) Bible college? What if you financed a new van, a youth-room makeover, or a special trip. One smaller church offers an all-expense paid "senior" vacation for graduates (who are church members) to some exotic location.

We mustn't forget our mission is to evangelize, encourage, educate, and equip children to discover, follow, and grow in Jesus. Sometimes the wisest financial choice a smaller church can make is to discontinue an expensive, ineffective program (no matter how long the tradition) or forego hiring a new youth/children's minister. At other times, however, the best thing a congregation can do is to hire additional staff, buy a computer, purchase a projection unit, invest in an innovative curriculum, or build new classrooms.

It is tough for smaller churches to effectively manage the money they have now, and the future may prove to be even more difficult. The past few decades have revealed some troubling financial trends. Even though personal family income maintains a modest growth, church offering plates are gathering fewer dollars every week. Personal bankruptcy in America has become a norm. Housing markets have softened and stagnated. Corporate layoffs, downsizing, and outsourcing forecast a looming financial crisis.

What does this mean to smaller churches? Essentially, it's crucial to develop wise coping strategies that provide successful ministry without financially draining the congregation. Smaller churches may also need to lead the way in revealing an attitude of "contentment" with fewer programs, leaner budgets, and scaled-down staff. In doing so, they might discover the advantage of doing less but doing it better.

SPENDING WISELY

A major expense for smaller churches is their children's curricula. Unfortunately, some congregations waste more than is necessary for effective Christian education.

Many resource rooms in small churches contain unused, dated student papers, extra craft boxes, and dried out, capless markers and glue sticks. Much of this waste could have been avoided through proper evaluation of supplies, effective ordering, and dedicated resource management.

A children's ministry can save bundles just by thinking ahead. When it's time to order student books or take-home papers, think 75 percent. That is, order enough for the students who attend three-quarters of the time. For example, a Sunday school class roll may have sixteen students listed, but perhaps only ten attend regularly. The proper order would be for twelve students (75 percent of sixteen). Another good idea is to purchase curriculum that doesn't rely on student books or take-home papers (unless reproducible). The savings will be significant, especially over time.

The only exception to this rule is Vacation Bible School. Since such programs are brief in nature, they require an "order of faith." Even so, evaluation of past VBS attendance, current children's population, and growth goals can make for a more accurate curriculum order.

It's also vital that smaller churches manage their resources properly. A little preventative maintenance—such as locking the door to the supply closet to keep classroom resources safe and secure—will save big bucks over time. Cataloging all church DVDs/videos and program resources initially takes time but the benefit of not having to replace a misplaced video is priceless.

Sometimes mismanaged resources can also cost time. I remember my personal frustration one Sunday morning when I arrived in my classroom to find someone had removed the DVD player (despite a sign that cautioned otherwise!). I lost more than twenty minutes running down a replacement. Consequently, policies and procedures for managing, moving, or requesting a needed resource should be developed.

Keep your storage areas and classrooms free from the clutter of used materials. Unless you have a specific plan for unused, dated curricula, it should be tossed (or better yet, donated to a smaller church!). Some churches are convinced that saving curriculum for the next round (three to four years later) is wise, but since many curriculum companies routinely evaluate, edit, and revise lessons, it's not all that thrifty.

> *Look at the staying power of your investment and the effect it will have in the lives of your church's children.*

See if you can simplify the scope of your program without losing effectiveness. A four-page monthly (paper) newsletter is nice, but would a brief (electronic) bi-weekly e-newsletter be a better choice? A church Web site—especially for children's ministry—is one of the first places would-be visitors go to learn about your church. What impression are you making? A Web site is infinitely more far-reaching than even a church sign, so why are many church Web sites outdated, boring, and loaded with errors? Is professionally-delivered pizza necessary, or would frozen or home-made pizza be just as enjoyable?

Sometimes a children's ministry should seek frugal solutions such as the ones mentioned above. At other times, a large expenditure may be a wise investment. For example, a set of children's ministry training DVDs may seem expensive, but its opportunity for multiple usage pays dividends. Paying for your children's ministry volunteers to attend a local training workshop may be expensive on paper, but what price can you put on an inspired, idea-filled, motivated volunteer? So look at the staying power of your investment and the effect it will have in the lives of your church's children.

DETERMINING PRIORITIES

Because of cost restrictions, you may not always accomplish everything you desire. Consequently, the leadership of a children's ministry must decide what's most important. You must discern the best allocation of resources, whether it involves new programming, curricula, or some other worthy effort. Sometimes, and often to our detriment, financial decisions in the smaller church are rooted in tradition. Change the curriculum? No chance. Denominational loyalty or comfort zones win that battle. Purchase background checks? It's not necessary. Ignorance and apathy answer until there's a real problem (by then it's too late!). Such shortsightedness can bind and blind a congregation from being more effective.

Always remember that programs, philosophies, and resources are only means to an end. Our goal is to lead each child into a relationship with Jesus that lasts a lifetime. Sometimes we need to be flexible and creative and to learn to forego some things we desire. As Paul encouraged the Philippian church, we must learn to be content regardless of our circumstances, to trust God to supply our needs, and to remember that through Christ we "can do everything."

TOP TEN WAYS FOR CUTTING THE BUDGET

(WITHOUT HURTING YOUR MINISTRY TO CHILDREN)

10. Use learning materials that can be reproduced. This allows for flexibility when class size changes.

9. To cover costs, charge nominal admission prices ($1–$2) at parties or special events.

8. Survey the congregation to find special abilities and talents (such as clowning, balloon art, Web design, magic, music, and drama) and resources (such as farms, vans, swimming pools, and video games).

7. Inform parents of special supply requests for items, such as paper towels, baby wipes, markers, scissors, CD players, TVs.

6. Hold a classroom shower. Encourage adults to contribute toys, supplies, and resources to equip the room for learning. Top off the shower with testimonies from the children and refreshments.

5. Send a monthly e-mail to congregational members noting a "Top 10 Needs for Our Children's Ministry." Post the list on your church's Web site. Send thank-you notes signed by the children to donors.

4. For correspondence, create homemade postcards from heavy paper and rubber stamps (available through any craft store). They're less spendy than professional cards, fun to create, and enjoyable to receive.

3. Use restaurants, schools, and malls for special activities. Treat the children to sodas at a fast-food restaurant known for its jungle gym wing.

2. Create your own crafts for VBS and other activities. Craft kits purchased from publishers can eat up half the total cost of a VBS budget. Seek out "crafty" people in your church and encourage them to create simple, yet fun, crafts that follow the VBS theme. Be sure they have plenty of time (at least two months) to create crafts and secure supplies.

1. Subscribe to a children's ministry resource magazine or Internet Web site. The ideas, programming helps, and encouragement will save hours, dollars, and sweat. It's the best bang for a subscription buck you'll ever find. Suggestions? Check out www.kidology.org, www.kidzmatter.com, and www.childrensministry.com.

THINKING OPPORTUNITY

A nearly unlimited bonanza of ministry resources awaits the determined smaller-church children's worker. To find and enjoy these opportunities, it's important to value patience, creativity, and persistence. Every obstacle is an opportunity. Every problem is a possibility.

Aaron understands this principle. He's a part-time children's choir director in an inner-city church of 90. He wanted to develop a choir for kids in the surrounding neighborhood and even hoped to tour with them. The problem was money. He had many interested children and parents, but little to no extra funds to do much else.

Aaron needed a set of risers for performances. He also knew a sound system and portable keyboard would be equally advantageous. On a larger scale, a van for transportation would solve tour issues. Aaron knew his needs and was willing to wait on his wants. The answer was to get creative.

It wasn't long before Aaron's explorations paid dividends. First, a retired carpenter in his church was willing to build portable risers, donating both time and materials. Then, with a few e-mails, Aaron located a keyboard and sound system. A couple of area churches were willing to loan them for performances, and one was considering a wholesale donation. Aaron arranged to have performances at both churches. A nearby children's home agreed to lend Aaron's group a van as long as basic expenses were covered. Aaron's own congregation, upon hearing these inspiring revelations, donated funding for all insurance needs. Aaron's new children's choir was ready to roll.

All smaller churches can find resources like Aaron did. It's amazing what's available when you simply ask. Begin with your own congregation. Does anyone have the skills or the resources to meet a need? a swimming pool? a laptap to load Power-Point? entertainment services? professional services (e.g., printing, food)? You'll be surprised what people will donate if they value your vision. In my first youth ministry, I created a special post-VBS party and field trip event for the children. Funds were tight and so I asked around for suggestions. I learned of a fringe member who owned a local fast-food restaurant. When approached, he was so excited that he donated full meals to over 100 children! A retired bus driver offered to bus the children to the event. Still another individual served as VBS photographer.

Auctions, yard sales, and thrift stores can be gold mines for great used stuff. Keep your eyes peeled for educational supplies, Christian music and books (hopefully not this one!), electronics, nursery toys (new only) and equipment (rockers, bins, art), and anything else your ministry needs.

Local business can also help. In many larger cities, special warehouses (e.g., Costco, Sam's Club) sell bulk items at wholesale prices. You can save a bundle on everything from paper plates to pencils to pizzas. Furthermore, some businesses owned by Christians will give special discounts to churches. And while churches shouldn't expect special treatment, it's a blessing when these businesses will work with you. One theater owner gave my children's ministry a flat ticket price for matinees that was a dollar cheaper. A print shop gave an extra 10 percent break on my flyers.

The possibilities to stretch the dollar are endless. Pursue each one passionately.

RAISING FUNDS

Fundraising is a common smaller-church technique and, frankly, it can be tiresome. Fundraisers are especially challenging for smaller congregations who rely upon fewer people to help and even contribute supplies, baked goods, or time. Surprisingly, a good chunk of the funds raised usually comes from the church people themselves! This reduces a children's ministry to begging from its own. And if most of the money is from outsiders, then that births a different question: Do you really want your children's ministry funded by nonmembers?

Many smaller churches prohibit any type of fundraising, citing Jesus' anger over money changers in the temple. Nevertheless, from time to time, it's both prudent and possible to hold a worthy fundraiser.

Here are some surefire FUNdraisers guaranteed to get the job done in the smaller church. Each idea is easily accomplished with just a few kids and none require much money upfront. They're designed to involve adults and children, together in ministry. And they're fun too!

• **Diving for Dollars.** This hot summer fundraiser will be a cool treat for children. An outdoor private pool works best (with a good section three to five feet deep). Several weeks prior to the event, encourage adults in Bible classes to contribute silver-colored coins (quarters, dimes, nickels, half-dollars, silver dollars) to "pool" together a fund.

On the day of the pool event, evenly spread the coins across the bottom of the pool. (Pools with bottom filters should be avoided for this activity!) Give each child participant a plastic cup and line kids up around the pool. On the signal, the kids jump in and find the treasure. Let the winner pass out chocolate candy coins to the other participants. Another variation is to form teams for a competition. Either way, this is a cool way to raise funds. And don't forget to invite the adults . . . they'll love to watch this one!

Remember that safety comes first. Avoid too many children participating at the same time. If necessary, you can always dump previously-retrieved coins back in for another round. It's all about the fun.

• **Pennies for Heaven.** Pennies are often thought of as small and insignificant change. But when added together, pennies can mean big bucks. Over a one-month period, collect pennies from adults and children. Encourage classes to wage friendly "penny-collecting" battles (adults vs. adults, kids vs. kids).

To chart your progress, have contributors trade in every sixty-six pennies for a mock Bible that can be taped to a wall. Try to cover the whole wall in Bibles. This is a great fundraiser to purchase real Bibles for a mission.

• **Pastoral Heights.** Similar to Pennies for Heaven, this fundraiser uses quarters instead of pennies. The object is for classes or teams of adults and children to create stacks of quarters as tall as the pastor. Since quarters are more valuable than pennies, the earning potential here is far greater (especially if your preacher is blessed with height!). All quarters become donations to the children's ministry program or to a designed project.

• **Trade Up.** Similar to a scavenger hunt, this moneymaker is both fun and can produce some grand results. Give each child a penny with a simple challenge: Find someone who will "trade up" with you. A penny for a nickel. A nickel for a dime. A $50 bill for $51 or $60 or whatever! The only guideline is a single contributor may not give twice to the same person and each child may only contribute once themselves to their own fund. One smaller church played this game with only ten children and together they raised over $3,000!

• **Super Subs and Soda.** Super Bowl Sunday is the perfect day for children to make a little dough: sub sandwiches and sodas, that is! For several weeks prior to the big game, have the children give super-sale announcements in worship services and take orders for sandwiches and sodas. Then purchase or make the sub sandwiches to fill the orders. Have extra sandwiches on hand for those appetites "made to order" on the day of the big game. Set up a table or booth and have people pick up their meals after church. Depending on overhead expenses, this fundraiser can earn a few hundred dollars.

Another winning combination is muffins and coffee. Adults will have to make the hot drinks, but kids can help set up and sell the goods. A good twist for both is to operate from a donation-only basis, as these tend to always bring in a larger return.

• **Wipe a Window.** Here's a fun service project for kids to do during worship hour. You'll need plenty of old newspapers, window cleaner, paper, pens, and envelopes. Simply send the children out to the church parking lot to clean side windows on cars. (Teens and adults will be needed to reach front and back windows.)

When finished, leave notes and small envelopes on the cars. The note should say something like: "Here's looking at you! The children of (name of church) need your help, and we've cleaned your windows to improve your vision about our needs. We're raising funds right now for (name of project) and thought you might *see* it in your heart to give. The envelope is provided for your gift and convenience."

• **Christmas Causes.** Have the children erect and decorate a Christmas tree (for a unique twist, do this in July!). On the tree, place small tags that describe needs in your children's ministry. The needs can be small (diapers for the nursery) or large (TV, projection unit). Hang as many tags as possible on the tree. Include programming costs, such as summer camp scholarships, DVDs for children's church, magazine subscriptions, and teacher-training conferences.

Encourage each family or individual to select a tag and purchase the item as a Christmas gift to the children's ministry. Place the contributions (wrapped) beneath the tree and be sure to send thank-you notes to all donors.

• **Money Scavenger Hunt.** Here's a fun Sunday evening event. Encourage families to come prepared to give (no more than $20)—in loose change and no more than $5 in one-dollar bills.

Provide fun prizes for the winners in each round: packets of flower seeds, candied popcorn, movie tickets, coupons to entertainment venues, and so on.

To play: Simply call out a specific amount of money (for example $1.62). The first family to produce that amount (nicely laid out on a table) wins the round, contributes the money, and takes home the prize. You can also have families hunt for the oldest coin, birth years of family members, and the dumpiest $1 bill. Pass an offering plate at the end of the evening and encourage families to contribute one final time.

Of course, there are countless possibilities for raising a few extra funds for your children's ministry. Personally, I think a good fundraiser will either be attractive (lots of fun) or rooted in service (to give purpose). Creativity is also important. How many car wash fundraisers do you visit? Unless your own kid is doing the soaping, it's just not a high priority. However, innovative fundraisers attract and usually produce better profits.

Ultimately, money matters to a smaller church. You may only have a couple mites, but in the hands of God that's a mighty offering.

You don't need a million dollars to change children.

Just change children.

CHILDREN'S MINISTRY BUDGET

A budget for children's ministry helps you organize your program, establish priorities, and define your overall purpose. Here's a possible financial breakdown for a church of one hundred with fifteen children (newborn through fifth grade). This budget encompasses all areas of children's ministry, from curriculum to camp scholarships. As described, this budget is lean with few frills. A good rule is to budget from $50–$100 per child per year. This budget of $1100 is a median amount for a church of this size ($75 per child per year). Use the space provided to make calculations and create your own children's ministry budget.

Resources/Training $500

- Music $25   _____
- Volunteer Training $75   _____
- Resource Materials $75   _____
- Curriculum $325   _____
- Other: _____

Activities/Programming $600

- Preschool Program $100   _____
- Children's Program $100   _____
- Family Ministry $100   _____
- Children's Church $150   _____
- Camp Scholarships $150   _____

Expenses $100

- Equipment $50   _____
- Publicity/Postage $50   _____
- Other: _____   _____

CHAPTER **8**

Teaching with Power

> *"Only be careful, and watch yourselves closely so that you do not forget the things your eyes have seen or let them slip from your heart as long as you live. Teach them to your children and to their children after them."*
>
> (DEUTERONOMY 4:9)

My grandma had a favorite saying, "Dynamite comes in small packages." She should know. At five foot-nothing, her small wiry frame packed a punch in passion, persistence, and patience.

My grandma with a wooden spoon was a lethal disciplinary weapon. I once saw her take on a muscle-bound hulk of a man nearly two feet taller than her just because he used offensive words around children. As a "mountain woman," Grandma could out-hike, out-pack, and out-work most people many times her junior. On her seventieth birthday, only two months before her death, she went waterskiing.

"It's not the dog in the fight," Grandma would also say, "it's the fight in the dog."

If there was one thing worth fighting for, to Grandma, it was Jesus. She voraciously read, interpreted, and taught the Scriptures. Her Bible was marked with copious notes from commentary research, sermon insights, or the teachings of other Christians. My earliest boyhood memory involves going to Bible study with her. I learned to love the Word myself while sitting with adults in a Wednesday Bible study. Grandma not only knew Scriptures, she could teach them with power. She once started a Bible study for teens in her home because our small home church was losing influence with the kids. In a few short months, her study was packed with teens. Oh, and she was around sixty-five years old at the time.

If there was one thing that bothered Grandma, it was "living a life without the Lord."

Grandma lived and taught . . . with power.

It's a lesson worth learning for the smaller church and its children's ministries. For most churches, especially smaller ones, Christian education is failing. A whole generation has emerged that is biblically-ignorant and spiritually-anorexic. In the last twenty years, children's and youth ministries have had better resources, better training, and better budgeting, and yet, few who graduate with a church education will last.

A 2007 LifeWay Research study of over a thousand Protestants between 18–30 years of age reveals that seven in ten individuals who "went to church regularly in high school" have stopped going to church by age twenty-three.[1] According to Dan Kimball, in his work, *They Like Jesus, but Not the Church*, one megachurch college pastor informed him that only one of every three teens who participated in their church's youth ministry and who remained in the area following graduation still attended church.[2]

Smaller church or mega congregation, this generation is walking away.

If this was public education, there would be referendums, deep analysis, revolutionary calls for change, media attention, and political plays to correct the problem.

But this is "church" and *Christian* education.

(Incidentally, of the one-third who stayed with church in their twenties, the primary reasons were that it brought vitality to their relationship with God and it served to aid daily decisions about life.[3])

A whole generation has emerged that is biblically-ignorant and spiritually-anorexic.

But here's the real dinger: where does this staying "power" have its genesis? Is there a period where what happens *now* will impact *then*? Related research, primarily by George Barna, suggests those who remain faithful in adulthood were persuaded to make commitments as preteens. I doubt there's a more crucial developmental period than ages ten to twelve. With the onset of abstract thought, puberty, and peer relationships, this brief window in time probably frames a person for life in values, choices, commitments, attitudes, and even behaviors.

Smaller-church children's ministries should particularly target their work with preteens and enlist quality volunteers to teach, lead, and love this age group. Failure at this age may mean lives lost to Christ.

POWER UP

Think about small stuff that's possessed with power. A seedling can grow into a mighty tree. A small stress fracture deep in the earth creates powerful, damaging earthquakes. The average cell phone has more power and computing abilities than the first rocket that sent man to the moon. The difference between a towering homerun and a weakly pop out can be measured in milli-seconds and micro-inches.

To teach with power is no different.

If we're going to change the course of a generation and charge the faith of children for a lifetime, it starts in the classroom. Too many teachers, especially in the smaller church, are apathetic, unprepared, and uncaring about the children they serve and the Scriptures they teach. I don't want to sound overcritical on this point. I know many smaller-church volunteers are stressed from wearing too many hats. And many are doing the best they can, considering the amount of training they have had. But when we're given the opportunity to teach God's Word to children, we accept a higher responsibility (Luke 17:1-3; James 3:1).

Think about it. If every smaller church simply focused on teaching God's Word with power to children, and since nearly nine in ten churches are "smaller" churches, imagine how a generation could be changed!

Recently our family drove into the mountains outside Boise. My son, for whatever reason, wanted to bring home a rock. As a joke, I chided him and said, "Now, son, if every person took home a rock from this mountain, there would be no more mountain." That quip led to dozens of parody comments like "if every person took a cup of air home from this mountain, there'd be no air up here."

You see, there's power in even the smallest act, including moving a mountain. I recognize that not every smaller church will sense the call to teach with power and not every leader who reads this work will desire to change, but if a few do—even many—then imagine the powerful change that could happen.

So how do you teach children with power?

In college, my homiletics professor made a powerful statement. It's so potent that in five years of ministry training—with hundreds of homilies and thousands of lectures—I remember vividly only this single mantra for creating a memorable sermon. I even recall the passionate delivery of the quote by my professor, whose eyes lit with fire and his voice rose with passion as he shared the homiletic advice of an old African American preacher:

First, I reads myself full.

Then, I thinks myself clear.

Then, I prays myself hot.

Then I lets myself go!

The secret to a good sermon is here, but it's also the recipe for teaching children effectively and with power.

PREPARATION ("FIRST, I READS MYSELF FULL.")

The average Sunday school teacher spends less than a half hour every week in lesson preparation. This lack of proper preparation explains why classes run wild with discipline problems, why children fail to learn biblical truth, and why many kids find church boring.

After all, if you don't prepare, you will repair.

It's that simple. Master teachers have long learned that preparation is what separates the ordinary instructor from the excellent educator in the classroom. Preparation is the legwork. It's the sweat equity. It's the pain that produces eventual gain.

For those who want to teach with power, there are three primary areas to prepare prior to the actual teaching event.

First, you need to prepare your lesson. I humbly recommend that no teacher, especially in the smaller-church setting, be allowed to write her own lessons. Why? Because few know how to develop lessons with effective objectives, solid sequencing, insightful questions, creative learning activities, and useful take-home materials. In fact, I've found that most teachers who pen their own lessons—regardless of their expertise—on the whole create a weaker lesson than even the most average curriculum choice available.

It's the time factor kicking in. I learned this lesson, personally, when I moved to writing professional church curriculum. A lesson that I would have taught my children in church demanded countless more hours of work to be accepted on the professional market. I realized that my stubbornness (and even ignorance) sometimes prevented me from teaching a better lesson. With other responsibilities that often took priority, I didn't have time to write as good of a lesson every week.

In fact, even today, as an experienced educator, I use a curriculum to teach. Why? Because it alleviates the pain in preparation. All I have to do is master the material. You should know your lesson so well you can leave your manual at home. It also gives me more time to prepare the physical classroom for learning and to gather supplies.

RESOURCES ▲ SPOTLIGHT

Here's a list of recommended curriculum companies and their Web sites, in no particular order, save alphabetical.

College Press Publishing—www. collegepress.com (1-800-289-3300)

David C. Cook Publishing—www. davidccook.com (1-800-323-7543)

Gospel Light Publishers—www. gospellight.com (1-800-4-GOSPEL)

Group Publishing—www.group.com (1-800-447-1070)

Standard Publishing—www.standardpub. com (1-800-543-1353)

As you seek a good curriculum for your Christian education program, ask these publishers to send samples of their curricula to you (most will give you a free sample) and request a "scope and sequence" to evaluate what topics (and in what order) will be taught.

Preparation of lessons was so important to me, as a leader of Christian education in one church, that I would call my teachers on Tuesday nights to ask for prayer needs, lesson supplies, and other matters needed for the upcoming Sunday. My teachers learned to review their lessons prior to my call and, in fact, most started preparing for the next Sunday as early as Monday. No more Saturday specials!

Teachers who enter the classroom fully prepared and ready (even with backup plans for unforeseen circumstances) will not only enjoy teaching more, they will also discover they're truly making a difference.

A second area of preparation is the learners themselves. Another reason to use a purchased curriculum is you're now free to prepare your students for Sunday or Wednesday night. I've often lamented that I'd love to invent a special set of goggles that allowed me to see the "emotional baggage" on my students' backs. Every learning experience happens with that baggage in tow, large and small. Mom and Dad fighting on the way to church. Family financial pressures. Grandpa is dying. The family pet is sick. An illness is causing displeasure. A bully at school is making pain. A teacher is overly critical. When you think about it, there's a lot of stuff a kid can haul into class—most of which you never see.

In fact, master teachers recognize the majority of behavioral problems are rooted either in belonging issues (the child isn't fitting in), boredom (teaching methods aren't working), or inner beliefs (how a child views himself). Both belonging and belief issues usually involve emotional baggage in the classroom. Consequently, it is important to take time to prepare yourself and your learners for the lesson by unpacking the "bags." Spend time sharing and caring and praying. Watch for children wearing their emotions on their sleeves. Invest in the lives of your kids outside of class (yes, this is preparation). Go to their games, their performances, and their homes. A prepared lesson is half-taught if the learner has been half-caught by you. You'll win their affection and attention if you give yours first.

A prepared lesson is half-taught if the learner has been half-caught by you.

A final area to prepare is your own life. The first person you teach your lesson to is *you.* The lesson must soak your heart and change your life before you'll cause any good in the kids on Sunday morning. Consequently, you shouldn't ask a child to do anything you wouldn't do. Want kids to memorize a verse? You better have it down first. Want them to think about something deeper? Are you considering it yourself? Want them to change and live differently? How has the lesson changed you?

You may notice that I've spent a lot of time explaining preparation. That's because great preparation involves soaking it with time. Even in this chapter.

And remember, if you don't prepare, you will repair. I guarantee it.

POINT ("THEN, I THINKS MYSELF CLEAR.")

Nothing is more exhausting in a classroom than the "content dump." If you've gone to college, you know the drill. The first day of class, the professor walks in and hands out the syllabus (which explains the forthcoming "dumping"). The rest of the semester resembles a large dump truck backing up to the minds of learners to "fill" them with what they need to know. And for many professors, the learners need to know a lot. After so many weeks, to evaluate what is "sticking," there is an exam. The more content a student can dump back on the page (I affectionately call it "academic vomit"), the better the grade. At the end, a final regurgitation happens and the final grade is issued accordingly.

The professor says he has taught well.

The student is happy, if it's a high grade.

So what's really been learned? What really stuck? You'd be surprised. After all, learning is what's left after the facts are forgotten. And for many kids—whether church or school—what's left is a bad attitude about the experience. Real learning changes lives. Use it or lose it, I say.

And that's my point here.

Powerful teaching doesn't flood the learner with meaningless material nor does it dump just to dump. Nothing is more dangerous than an educated educator who's more in love with what he knows than how to communicate and transfer his knowledge effectively.

Master teachers boil down the material for memorable points. You've seen it in this book, I hope. Sometimes it's a powerful metaphor, story, or illustration. Sometimes it's an engaging question. Sometimes a simple statement like "if you don't prepare, you'll repair."

Nearly every printed curriculum will already have a primary lesson aim. This is your point. For example, it might be: "The children will appreciate the love of Jesus." So that's what you hit, over and over and over again. In every question, in every story, in every learning activity, you lead the children to "appreciate the love of Jesus." You pound it, you proclaim it, you propagate it roundly. If you do, your class should leave tattooed with "the love of Jesus."

Got the point?

Good, let's move on.

PRAYER ("THEN, I PRAYS MYSELF HOT.")

I'm amazed at how little time teachers spend in prayer (myself included). The act of prayer connects us to a greater power than we can even imagine. Just take the time to investigate the life of Christ and you'll see a regular commitment to communicate with the Father.

We can prepare our lessons, our learners, and our lives.

We can manage our learning content into memorable moments.

But if we fail to pray, all our preparation is empty. "Unless the LORD builds the house," Solomon once penned, "its builders labor in vain" (Psalm 127:1). Prayer is not an add-on thing. It's not an afterthought or a pregame blessing. Prayer should infuse the whole learning process.

We should pray before we ever open the teaching manual to review next week's lesson. We should pray as we're reviewing it, asking for additional insight and ideas. We should pray for our children to receive the lesson, enjoy the lesson, and live the lesson. We should pray that our lesson time is not impacted by disruption, discipline problems, or other distractions. We should pray that our hearts are ready to teach this lesson. We should pray daily. We should pray as we enter the classroom and even while class is in session. We should pray out loud, silently, through song, in service, and regardless of the hour. Finally, when the lesson is over and the kids are gone, we should thank God for showing up in spite of our weakness, failures, and mistakes.

Make no mistake: if you want to teach with power, you'll need to be connected to the Source "who is able to do immeasurably more than all we ask or imagine, according to his power that is at work within us" (Ephesians 3:20).

PASSION ("THEN, I LETS MYSELF GO.")

Nothing is more powerful than a passionate teacher. He's insightful and informative, entertaining and engaging. A powerful, passionate teacher can fuel empty minds, fire apathetic hearts, and forge purposeless lives. Sometimes we call such teachers "enthusiastic," and that's correct. The word *enthusiasm* is rooted in two Greek words: *en* (or "in") and *theos* (or "God"). Technically, when we're "enthusiastic" about something, we are "in God." We've tapped into that higher power that makes us more than we can ever imagine or even ask.

When I think of passion, I think of fire in the heart. Ironically, throughout the Scriptures, the presence of God is as "fire." The burning bush. The fire by day to lead the Israelites. Three men in a fiery furnace with a fourth [man]. Elijah's fire from Heaven and fiery chariot. Tongues of fire on Pentecost. God is called "a consuming fire" (Hebrews 12:29), while Jesus' eyes are described as "blazing fire" (Revelation 1:14).

Passion, like fire, is uncontrollable. It's wild. It's majestic. It's also very powerful. It purges and cleanses, it releases and frees, and it changes everything. Teachers who are "on fire" will change lives. They will be unpredictable (never boring). They will be fun. They will be attractive. And they remove ignorance, prejudice, and arrogance. Ultimately they'll burn their own lives into the souls of their students.

If you've been around a fire—especially a large one—you know you walk away smelling of smoke. Sometimes it's so ingrained in the fabric, you can't wash it out. You can't remove it. The memory of that fire is so deep in the threads that one sniff takes you back.

Imagine in twenty years that a new statistic emerges in America. Imagine that for some reason young adults no longer leave the church. They can't. Their Christianity is so burned into their souls, psyches, and value systems that it can't be erased. It can't be washed out by worldly desires. It can't be removed by painful crisis. It can't be lost to tradition, trial, or time. Just one sniff and it takes them back.

Imagine in two decades that a whole generation exists unwilling to walk on, fall away, or leave behind their faith. That would be a powerful day!

Imagine if this strength of faith was rooted in thousands of smaller churches who simply said it's time to teach "with power" the children of our congregations to love and follow Jesus. Imagine this faith so strongly forged in these churches that by age thirteen countless teens continued to mature as believers to the point where they refused—even to death—to deny the Christ they followed.

Imagine the power of a Christian generation released to evangelize, educate, and equip others to follow the Jesus they love. That would be a powerful generation!

Imagine the change in future families, communities, and even whole nations. Imagine a world turned upside down. That would be a powerful time in history!

Teachers who are "on fire" will change lives.

And it's all because teachers finally realized their responsibility, properly prepared, purposely targeted, incessantly prayed, and passionately taught the Scriptures.

Go ahead, imagine. Then teach.

Teach for all *your* worth.

Like Grandma said, "Dynamite comes in small packages."

It's time to light the fuse.

Teaching to Produce Learning: Infants

Moral Development: Infants are really in a stage of "premoral" development, but that doesn't mean they can't learn right and wrong. Because language skills are primitive (and nonexistent in babies), infants respond to their environments by pleasure or pain.

Cognitive Level: Babies and toddlers are very primitive thinkers. They learn via their senses, especially taste and touch.

Concepts to Be Learned:
- God is good.
- God is love.
- Church is a good, safe place.
- God made me.

Teaching Children: Think A-B-C-D!
A = Attitudes (Babies/Toddlers)
B = Beliefs (Preschoolers)
C = Commitments (Ages 7–9)
D = Decisions (Preteens)

Teaching to Produce Learning with . . .	Teaching Methods	Learning Experiences
1 Child	free play, blocks, toy animals, rockers, swings, roller toys, fuzzy Bibles	free play with blocks and other nursery toys, singing to the infant, holding the infant (especially in discomfort), changing diapers and providing simple snacks, reading simple cloth books
1–5 Children	free play, blocks, toy animals, rockers, swings, roller toys, fuzzy Bibles	free play with blocks and other nursery toys, singing to the infant, holding the infant (especially in discomfort), changing diapers and providing simple snacks, reading simple cloth books
5–10 Children	free play, blocks, toy animals, rockers, swings, roller toys, fuzzy Bibles	free play with blocks and other nursery toys, singing to the infant, holding the infant (especially in discomfort), changing diapers and providing simple snacks, reading simple cloth books

TEACHING TO PRODUCE LEARNING: AGES 3–6

Moral Development: Preschoolers are very "me-oriented." They are the center of their own worlds. Their entire view of right and wrong—along with their faith—is based upon what influential models (such as parents and teachers) tell them.

Cognitive Level: Preschoolers' play is symbolic of real life (e.g., playing house, driving a car).

Concepts to Be Learned:
- God loves us.
- God made the world.
- God sent Jesus to the world.
- We can love Jesus.
- We go to church to worship God.
- We can share and help others.
- We can say "Thank you."

Teaching Children: Think A-B-C-D!
A = Attitudes (Babies/Toddlers)
B = Beliefs (Preschoolers)
C = Commitments (Ages 7–9)
D = Decisions (Preteens)

Teaching to Produce Learning with . . .	Teaching Methods	Learning Experiences
1 Child	home living, art, books, blocks, puzzles, music	interactive play, book reading, neighborhood/nature walks, sing-along tapes/videos, coloring projects
1–5 Children	home living, art, books, blocks, puzzles, music	nature walks, group story times, free play with each other, sing-along tapes/videos for worship, group coloring projects, group paintings, modeling clay sculptures, stories on tape/video/DVD
5–10 Children	home living, art, books, blocks, puzzles, music	group story times, group coloring projects, modeling-clay sculptures, singing and finger plays, free play with each other, simple crafts, learning stations (painting, puzzles), stories on tape/video/DVD, group games (Duck, Duck Goose)

TEACHING TO PRODUCE LEARNING: AGES 7–9

Moral Development: For younger children, the moral code is "an eye for an eye." If they are pinched, they pinch back. Personal values are rooted in a "law and order" approach. Things that benefit young children are almost always seen as right, whereas harmful things are almost always viewed as wrong. The world, like their faith, is black and white.

Cognitive Level: Young children think in concrete terms about the ideas and concepts they're learning. They need help understanding symbols and abstract ideas (e.g., Jesus is the living water).

Concepts to Be Learned:
- We can make good decisions.
- We can talk to God.
- We can learn and follow God's ways and commandments.
- We can serve Jesus.
- God keeps his promises.

Teaching Children: Think A-B-C-D!
A = Attitudes (Babies/Toddlers)
B = Beliefs (Preschoolers)
C = Commitments (Ages 7–9)
D = Decisions (Preteens)

Teaching to Produce Learning with . . .	Teaching Methods	Learning Experiences
1 Child	art, books, blocks, puzzles, music	watercolor paintings, modeling-clay sculptures, neighborhood/nature walks, free play outside, reading of simple books, Bible memory activities, sing-a-long tapes/videos/DVDs, animated Christian videos/DVDs, field trips to parks/restaurants, puzzles, nature searches with magnifying glasses
1–5 Children	art, books, blocks, puzzles, music	watercolor paintings, modeling-clay sculptures, neighborhood/nature walks, free play outside, reading of simple books, Bible memory activities, puppet plays, crafts, small-instrument bands, dress-up fashion shows, field trips, singing
5–10 Children	home living, art, books, blocks, puzzles, music	watercolor paintings, modeling-clay sculptures, organized outside play, book centers, group Bible memory activities, video learning centers, group puzzles, group games (tag, Red Light/Green Light), puppet plays, crafts, small instrument bands, dress-up fashion shows, group singing

TEACHING TO PRODUCE LEARNING: AGES 10–12

Moral Development: Preteens begin to see shades of gray in their world. They question authority more and understand that individual values can impact the lives of others. They also begin to understand that doing "wrong things" (sinning) means more than just "getting in trouble" or facing punishment from parents or teachers. Faith becomes a working, personal faith.

Cognitive Level: Older children continue to think in concrete terms, although by the end of childhood they readily understand abstract concepts, including metaphor, simile, parody, and contradiction.

Concepts to Be Learned:
- We can live for God in today's world.
- We can understand the elements of the Christian faith.
- The church is important.
- We can improve relationships with our families and peers.

Teaching Children: Think A-B-C-D!
A = Attitudes (Babies/Toddlers)
B = Beliefs (Preschoolers)
C = Commitments (Ages 7–9)
D = Decisions (Preteens)

Teaching to Produce Learning with . . .	Teaching Methods	Learning Experiences
1 Child	art, drama, music, creative writing, oral communication, outreach opportunities, community builders	research projects (using Bible commentaries), arts and crafts, field trips/tours, letters to missionaries/pen pals, simple science experiments, object lessons, cooking/baking, write a play, song, newspaper column, etc.
1–5 Children	art, drama, music, creative writing, oral communication, outreach opportunities, community builders	research projects (using Bible commentaries), arts and crafts, field trips/tours, letters to missionaries/pen pals, group science experiments, object lessons, group cooking/baking, drama, puppets, create a video, write a play, song, newspaper column, etc.
5–10 Children	art, drama, music, creative writing, oral communication, outreach opportunities, community builders	team research projects (using Bible commentaries), age-appropriate crafts, missionary-support projects, team science experiments, object lessons, group dramas, puppet presentations, videotape Bible stories/parables, children's choirs, writing of plays and songs

CHAPTER 9

Kiss and Tell Worship

> *"Jesus said, 'Let the little children come to me, and do not hinder them, for the kingdom of heaven belongs to such as these.'"*
>
> (MATTHEW 19:14)

'll never forget the day I left my daughter in the hands of a college hundreds of miles away. No matter how hard I worked to hold back the tears, I found myself dancing on the edge of an emotional collapse. The memories of when I held Becca as a baby flooded my mind. I fondly recalled long walks at the zoo, backyard catch, and cross-country vacations. I have to admit I wanted to be a different type of father to my kids. I wanted to be emotionally expressive and unafraid to "kiss and tell." I wanted my children to know I loved them.

I also hoped they'd return the favor. Thankfully, they have.

Kisses, like worship, are not a solitary activity. It takes two to smooch, and worship inherently suggests a deep, intimate relationship—between God and man and within community.

Actually, worship is an interesting word. It sounds a bit odd too. In fact, depending on the cultural accent, it smacks a tad close to "war ship" (which, unfortunately, can also define the controversial context that this topic produces). The "worship wars" in many smaller churches are still being waged and, trust me, the children are watching.

Worship should be a bit messy, imperfect, and even risky.

The problem is rooted in the fact that worship is intensely personal. The music and lyrics that carry one person to the throne can cause another to leave the room. Whether it's a hymn, a chorus, a psalm, or song, preferences are widespread and opinions waxed strong. Whole churches, even movements and denominations, have split over music styles, instrumental use, and worship expressions.

Maybe that's why Jesus said those who truly discover the throne will be like little children. What's a tiny tot got over the experienced adult? Why would the kingdom of Heaven belong to kids? And why would Jesus even encourage children to come to him? After all, in his social setting, a child was more property than prospect, an individual who was to be silent and segregated.

Not much has changed in 2,000 years.

And that's Jesus' point to these adults: innocence, wonder, and risk are kingdom values. Children have them, naturally, and these values are at the heart of worship. In the context of Matthew 19, children were clamoring to be around the Christ. They enjoyed being near him and even climbing into his lap and arms. Personally, I think Jesus was famous for his hugs. And children love to be held.

It was a safe place then. It's still a safe place.

But I think there's something more too. Most children take a risk to crawl into an adult's lap. It requires effort, persistence, and even creativity. Sometimes they learn, halfway into the climb, that the adult doesn't want them to come further.

Or they find themselves swooped into the lap with a laugh. I think this is what Jesus found valuable in a child. Kids are willing to risk—even rejection—to experience the hug. Kids will keep climbing, and, at the core, is an innocence that marks the journey.

The Old Testament word for "worship" has multiple interpretative meanings, but one of my favorites equates worship to a "kiss." Worship is an intimate experience with a holy God where we "kiss" and connect. If you talk about kissing with kids, especially preteens, you'll discover most find the prospect ripe with "cooties" and "girl germs." But it is more than a romantic idea to worship God and "kiss" him. Intrinsically, it's more familial or parental in nature.

Most parents welcome a good-night kiss from their children. It prepares them for the greater parting later. When I finally said good-bye to my daughter, it was a sloppy moment. We stumbled over our words. We longed to linger just a moment more. We reminisced about special moments. A kiss—whether good-bye or good-night—says "I love you," but it also states "I care" and "I'm here."

Which is why I think God weeps over our worship wars.

I doubt He cares about the style of the "kiss," but I know He longs for the moment of connection. He anticipates the opportunity to say "I love you" and "I care" and "I'm here." God even loves "sloppy agape." Worship should be a bit messy, imperfect, and even risky. But like so many older children, who've outgrown kisses (in their own minds), we often reduce corporate worship to a set of rules, style, or performance. God looks for the kiss, and we give him a procedural peck. One smaller church I served back in the 1980s actually lost ten families when we switched from hymnals to an overhead projector! Another more recent example was a full-blown fight over PowerPoint and an electric guitar.

That's why this chapter on children and worship is so important.

If smaller churches would allow the little ones to guide and guard their worship philosophy, perhaps there'd be more kissing and less fighting. Kids welcome wonder, and at the core of worship is a commitment to an awesome God. Children enjoy risk and are tolerant of diversity, change, and preferences. The little ones also seek to experience God through their senses. They will stand, sit, kneel, smell, touch, listen, shout, and even enjoy the opportunity to "taste and see that the Lord is good." Imagine the revolution in adult worship if we allowed a little child to lead the way? It doesn't mean we'd like everything that happens, but it would create harmony and vision and values.

When it comes to children and worship, there are a few primary programming options: children in the adult worship service, self-contained children's church, and a hybrid between the two (where kids stay in worship for a portion of the service and then leave for a different teaching time). Let's examine each situation and dialogue about the advantages and disadvantages for each programming strategy.

CHILDREN IN ADULT WORSHIP

LaShawna is the type of kid who would get lost in a larger church. But in her congregation, she played a valuable role every Sunday.

It was a sweltering August Sunday, and LaShawna was just barely five years old. Nothing unusual happened (the norm for this small church of forty people in south Alabama) until about twenty-five minutes into the pastor's message. As the preacher launched into his final point, his voice cracked and, then, croaked. Literally. After several painful coughs, tears welled in the pastor's eyes, and everyone sat frozen waiting for the episode to end.

Everyone but LaShawna.

She was already gone to the church kitchen to retrieve a glass of water. Despite her small stature, LaShawna found a way to draw a cup of cold water and rushed back to hand the cup to the pastor. The grateful preacher drank every drop and then returned to his point and the text: "I tell you the truth, whoever gives you a cup of water in my name . . . will certainly not lose his reward" (Mark 9:41).

LaShawna didn't miss a Sunday after that day. The truth is, she couldn't. After the service, the pastor asked LaShawna if she'd consider drawing a glass of cold water as a weekly ministry for him. LaShawna beamed and replied, "No pwoblem." When LaShawna grew older, she handed the task to another younger child. To this day, a child supplies the preacher with a cold glass of water every Sunday. And, from time to time, especially when the southern air sweats with heat and humidity, the pastor will recount the story of the day LaShawna gave the water.

Funny, but no one seems to mind hearing it again.

LaShawna is now a mom herself and faithfully attends the little church with her own kids. She is also active in other areas of service, from teaching to secretarial work. It's not difficult to imagine that LaShawna's early act of service and the fact she was both welcomed and provided responsibility helped forge a faith that remains today. It's also notable that had she been in a larger church, maybe even a few dozen more, her act of service might not have happened or the opportunity would have been lost to an adult attendant. It definitely wouldn't have occurred in a larger congregation as many exclude children all together from the adult worship experience.

One of the real difficulties with adult worship is it's created by adults for adults. If children are allowed to participate, they usually must remain quiet and are largely ignored. Kids do learn, though, even in the most formal and adult of all worship experiences. But what they remember may not be the message we hope they harbor. Rather, many kids discover that "adult worship" is boring, irrelevant, long in time, and short in understanding. Big people with big words doing boring things.

LaShawna's early act of service and the fact she was both welcomed and provided responsibility helped forge a faith that remains today.

The good news is that worship doesn't have to be this way. The smaller church can easily create kid-friendly worship experiences that are far more attractive than larger churches. A smaller congregation has more room for kids to participate. The flexibility of a smaller church provides a more comfortable atmosphere for a child's initial attempts to lead. And the community spirit within the smaller church context lends for less embarrassment when children fuss, flop, or even fail.

To fully involve children in your worship experiences, it's helpful to consider their gifts, abilities, skills, and interests. How can you tap into those traits for more meaningful worship? When I was ten years old, my doodling on the back of church bulletins landed me an opportunity for a chalk talk in front of the whole congregation. As my minister preached on Heaven, I drew a pastel picture of the Christian's hope. It wasn't a Rembrandt and it didn't win a ribbon, but it hung in the church basement for years.

Another strategy for involving children in worship is through an object lesson or a children's sermon. Some churches do this weekly and others prefer a monthly tradition. In these mini-sermons, children gather around the pastor or another adult who shares a brief lesson for the children. I have found the Catholic tradition particularly helpful for involving children. In most Masses, children will help lead the priest to the altar, some holding crosses and one with a large Bible lifted above the head. Children are also "blessed" by the priest during the weekly Eucharist celebration. In fact, few churches involve children in the adult worship better than the Catholic faith.

A different spin that can involve children in worship is a fun idea called "sermon in a sack." Each week a different child brings an object hidden in a paper sack or box. The children gather around the pastor and the object is first presented and then revealed. The preacher—unaware of the object—must then connect a spiritual truth to the object in the bag. It's unpredictable, fun to watch, and educational. One smaller church actually held a "Sermon in the Sack" Sunday where the entire message was a series of object lessons from items the children brought to church.

Children can be involved through music and drama too. Few things bring more smiles than a child's toothless rendition of "Jesus Loves Me." And puppets bring out the kid in everyone. Older children can be encouraged to create PowerPoint shows set to Christian music. In fact, many older children could help design worship slides and even the PowerPoint for the sermon.

It's easy for children (as well as many unchurched adults) to be confused by church rituals, objects, and traditions. Therefore, be creative in explaining difficult concepts. A smaller congregation of 125 in central Kansas portrays an annual "Living Last Supper" to teach the congregation and guests the possible thoughts of the disciples the night prior to the crucifixion. Another church in Kansas City encourages every family who connects with their congregation to contribute a "cross" to the wall in the church entrance. Every cross has the family name engraved upon it, and the wall is a living legacy to the church through the years.

Consider using a video to involve kids in worship. Videotape children as they respond to theological questions (e.g., "What does God look like?") and then replay the video as an introduction to a sermon or service. A number of excellent children's worship videos exist that even adults will enjoy singing along with.

> *To fully involve children in your worship experiences, it's helpful to consider their gifts, abilities, skills, and interests.*

You can also use older children as readers and ushers. Kids can distribute bulletins, greet worshipers, and collect offerings. Older children can read short inspirational stories or announcements for future events. Kids can read Bible passages, responsive readings, or letters from missionaries. Even young children can recite verses they've learned. If you ask children to read something in worship, give them the material in advance and encourage them to practice it prior to service. This kind of involvement not only exposes children to the congregation and provides experience, but also helps them learn to speak in public.

Use special days to your advantage, especially Christmas, Easter, Mother's Day, and Father's Day. These holidays lend a natural opportunity to celebrate family, children, and parents. A small Kentucky church created a male choir for Mother's Day and vice versa for Father's Day. These choirs were open to anyone, regardless of age. It was a special moment to witness mothers with daughters and fathers with sons serenading the congregation with a favorite hymn. Christmas is a wonderful time to involve children. Allow children to help deck the halls and trim the tree. Create a living Nativity (using children and real animals) for the Christmas Eve service.

Many of these ideas will make your adult worship services more comfortable for children. But adult worship may not meet the need for a child to learn to love worship. And that's where the concept of a children's church is worth investigating.

CHILDREN'S CHURCH—MAKING IT WORK

Children's church is a key opportunity to build spirituality within kids and can contribute significantly to a total children's ministry program. In my experience, children's ministries that feature a powerful, life-changing children's church program naturally draw families, growth, and spiritual transformation.

A great children's church hour will draw children to other programs, including Sunday school, midweek meetings, and extracurricular activities.

Children's church traditionally operates during the same hour as an adult worship service. Consequently, it's prime-time children's ministry, since some families come to church for only a single hour. In fact, children's church may be the only time all week you'll see certain kids. That's why if there's one program that can set the tone for a whole children's ministry, it's kids' worship. Whereas a Vacation Bible School—good, poor, or in-between—can create favor or flight as a response to the event, a children's church is even more vital for weekly (or weakly) attendance by kids. A great children's church hour will draw children to other programs, including Sunday school, midweek meetings, and extracurricular activities.

But let me confess an observation: many smaller churches may not need to develop a separate children's church program. The key is the number of children your church might service during a children's worship hour. The heart of a children's church will be grades one through five, and if fifteen children cannot regularly populate a children's church service, it will struggle and even fail. For children to worship corporately, it's hard for a group smaller than fifteen to generate enthusiasm, volume, and power. Children simply feel too self-conscious to sing out if there aren't a lot of other kids present. It also creates issues in teaching and group work. Finally, volunteers will easily discourage and even bail feeling the problem is personal when, in reality, it's programmatic. Consequently, if your church cannot maintain a minimum fifteen children, then a full-service children's church will naturally falter and fail.

Another important consideration is the intentionality of this program. Why develop a children's church program anyway? In many churches, it can devolve into a glorified child-care session or "fun and games" hour. I've heard from many adults that children's church helps keep noisy children out of adult worship.

But ultimately the purposes of this program spell WORSHIP.

• **Worth—Kids matter to God.** They are valuable and demand more from programs than mere babysitting.

• **Ownership—Kids can lead.** They are able to contribute and, in fact, seek opportunities to make a difference and create change.

• **Relationships—Kids matter to each other.** Children need to learn social skills in order to relate to others, both now and in the future.

• **Salvation—Kids need God.** As statistical research has revealed, most individuals make their commitments to God and frame their perceptions of church by age thirteen.

• **Honor—Kids need to learn traditions.** A key ingredient for a children's church is to teach kids the distinctions, history, traditions, and rituals of your church.

• **Instruction—Kids need to be biblically literate.** A children's church can build a corporate biblical foundation that weaves multiple ages together and reinforces concepts learned in other programs.

• **Prayer—Kids need to learn to talk to God.** Few children learn how to pray at church. A children's church creates opportunity for kids to build an intimate prayer life.

I once interviewed several children and asked them to share what they would like adult worship leaders to know about them. Their answers were varied, but ultimately could be summarized by the following statements:

"We want to and can enter into worship."

"We want to be more physically involved in how we worship."

"We need real examples to understand complex themes."

"We need help in transitioning between worship activities."

"We need to understand our church's traditions."

"We need to worship with a sense of direction."

Foremost, children seek a children's church that values their desire to worship and not just play for an hour. Older children, in particular those seeking spiritually, want to initiate a deeper relationship with God. It's one of the reasons that larger children's churches recognize the importance of splitting K–3 from 4–5/6. If attendances and volunteer support allow, a two-tiered children's church is optimal. Younger children enjoy songs that are more basic, including old favorites like the "B-I-B-L-E" (yes, that's the book for me!), while preteens welcome worship that connects them to each other and to God (such as "Shout to the Lord" and "The Heart of Worship").

One of the primary reasons children break out into misbehavior in a children's church is a failure to create good transitions.

Secondly, children want to be more physically involved in worship. They enjoy songs that feature movement, whether jumping or clapping or raising their hands. Furthermore, kids welcome opportunities for physical contact with one another. Songs where they link arms, high five, or "shake a friend's hand" will be popular and helpful for bringing children into a worshipful spirit. Some children may need guidance in appropriate touch and incidences where physical actions intensify (e.g., hitting) shouldn't be tolerated.

Most children, especially younger ones, are concrete thinkers. Consequently you'll need to develop powerful metaphors to help kids understand abstract concepts. For example, the concept of the Trinity can be explained using water, ice, and gas ("three expressions, one element"). Or the reason we "lift Jesus on high" in worship could point to a billboard or tall business sign. Object lessons also are helpful in making the complex more simple and the abstract more concrete.

Effective transitions between songs, activities, and major program components are vital. One of the primary reasons children break out into misbehavior in a children's church is a failure to create good transitions. Silence. Awkward change from one activity to another. Moving from a fast-tempo song to a slow worship song. If the transition is choppy or stalls, children will naturally fill the quiet with noise, movement, or worse. It takes good planning and intentionality to iron out the wrinkles in transitions, but the results are obvious.

Children's church is probably the one program where church traditions, rituals, and history can be explained and exhibited. Every congregation is different and even new smaller-church plants are creating a living history, but every church has an inner genetic tradition. Some are doctrinal nuances (e.g., baptism, the Lord's Supper, worship). Others are historical moments that have marked the congregation. Still others are rich traditions unique to the local community and culture. Children need to understand and learn these congregational traditions, especially those that they'll need to carry into adulthood.

Finally, kids enjoy a worship experience with some sense of direction. A consistent time format is important. When selecting songs to sing, think of how they take the children toward something. Some songs are relational and encourage children to operate horizontally. Others are reflective and cause kids to go within themselves. Still others point the children to God in Heaven and bring them upward. A good worship service will be short (ten to twelve minutes) and encourage kids to go in one or more of these directions.

SPLIT-SERVICE CHILDREN'S CHURCH

A popular type of children's church program is the split-service. In this approach, children participate in the adult worship service through a particular point, usually leaving just prior to the preaching. Depending on the population of children who leave, this exodus can range from being mildly humorous to horrendously disruptive to the adult worship. The smaller the church, the easier it is to tolerate a split-service approach, but eventually the need to move a substantial number of children out of the adult worship space will prove difficult.

One advantage to split-service is it allows children to participate in worship with adults, including important church traditions such as offering and Communion. Another upside involves finding volunteers to assist. When children leave the worship service, they are a walking billboard saying, "We're going somewhere and we need help." For adults who are captivated by that calling, a split-service is relatively volunteer-friendly since the sermon is usually all but what's missed.

In my mind, however, I think there are more significant disadvantages. The act of children leaving church is disruptive, even if small in number. Adults, especially those without children, often find the exodus damaging to their own worship experience. Another disadvantage is what to do with the children once they're gone. By the time the children get to a different space and settle down, there's only about fifteen to twenty minutes worth of time before church releases. It's extremely difficult to find curriculum or learning ideas to match this brief time. Consequently, many split-service programs becomes child-care sessions where children just play, enjoy a snack, and receive a brief biblical thought.

Too many discipline techniques are reactionary. A better approach is to understand why kids misbehave and stop disruptive moments before they materialize.

The greatest disadvantage is the hidden message a split-service program sends the children spiritually. Few leaders think about this point. One hidden message is that children are unwanted in the adult worship experience. Another is that what's about to happen (preaching) isn't for kids. Still another is that the best answer to removal from adult worship is a game, a snack, recess, or a Bible lesson (which, if boring, is even worse). It's no wonder that many children who graduate from split-service children's churches tend to be more apathetic, uninvolved, and bored later. Split-services are easy fixes, especially for smaller churches, but ultimately they are not the best programming for children.

A WORD ABOUT DISCIPLINE

Discipline is a common frustration in children's church. One advantage for smaller congregations is the numbers. Fewer kids mean fewer problems.

Nevertheless, kids will be kids and that means some will be disruptive.

The question is not how to respond, but why the kids are misbehaving. Too many discipline techniques are reactionary. A better approach is to understand *why* kids misbehave and stop disruptive moments before they materialize.

Essentially, there are only three primary reasons why children misbehave. First, they act up due to "belonging" issues. They don't feel like they fit in. Psychologist Rudolf Dreikurs suggested every person has a genuine need to belong and when this need isn't met then "mistaken goals" are pursued. Initially, a child struggling to belong will seek attention through mostly innocent strategies, such as talking to a friend quietly, tapping a pencil, or saying something funny. If such actions don't work, the child graduates to power plays in which he intentionally works against the teacher/leader by talking loudly, interrupting, or hitting. If these power plays don't resolve the belonging issue, the child graduates to revenge tactics, such as open defiance, unwillingness to participate, or mean comments. Eventually, when revenge doesn't work, the child simply gives up. Quiet, yes. Compliant, to a point. Learning, no.

Dreikurs' model helps leaders to reconsider some discipline strategies. For example, a "time-out" is a common reactive tool. Put the kid in a corner until she can behave. But what does that accomplish to resolve a need to belong? In fact, it will actually drive a child from attention-getting to power plays and from power plays to revenge. And when we power play a child's power plays, it's a fruitless exercise.

153

Will you win? Sure. But you won't win affection or attention. Instead you'll reap anger and apathy.

A second reason for misbehavior is boredom. Kids who aren't connecting with the lesson will act up or out. Creative children especially can bore easily. And children with active learning styles also struggle, particularly with passive activities, such as lectures, videos, and even discussions. It's important to remember that predictability is the path to boredom. And be careful not to exhaust attention spans (just think their age: three years = three minutes, ten years = ten minutes). My education professor once quipped, "The mind can only absorb what the seat can endure." So keep activities moving, brief, and changing.

A final reason kids misbehave is inner beliefs. Many children are preprogrammed by parents, peers, and other significant people to act in certain ways. When you expect a child to misbehave, he will. Watch what you say to children. Avoid comments and questions like: "You can do this, your sister always did well." "Why can't you be good?" "You'll never get it right, will you?" When you frame a child's inner beliefs with unfair comparisons or expectations, you'll create a kid who emotionally walks with a limp.

A KISS IS STILL A KISS

Ultimately, children will most likely develop a mature faith within a full-service children's church (that meets separately from the adults) or as active participants within an adult worship experience. Children who discover how to worship God in power, truth, and intimacy will grow into adults who worship God in power, truth, and intimacy.

Worship is certainly like a kiss.

And most kisses are worth talking about.

Which reminds me, I need to call my daughter.

Drawing Children into the Sermon

It's fairly simple to make sermons more kid-friendly. But first, get to know your church's children. Interview them about their hobbies, interests, foods, favorite TV shows, favorite Web sites, music, and sports heroes. Eat pizza with them and watch a movie or a hit TV show they'll enjoy. Watch what makes them laugh. Play a game of basketball. Then you'll be better prepared to use these ideas that even your adults will enjoy.

• **In each message, use at least one illustration that children will understand.** Don't know if a story will work? Try it out on a few fourth-graders first. Do you want a point to be meaningful for kids? Illustrate it with objects, articles, and situations from a child's world.

• **Create sermon-time games.** Make up Bingo cards or word-search puzzles with key words from the week's sermon. Encourage the children to listen for the words and mark them appropriately on the game sheets.

• **Use objects to explain points.** Preaching a sermon about the Light of the World? Preach by candlelight. Talking about sin? Deliver your message beside a garbage can of smelly trash. Get a haircut as you tell the story of Samson.

• **Watch your language.** Leave your dictionary at the door. Words such as "propitiation" and "sanctification" sound scholarly but leave children (and most adults) confused and clueless. If you're referring to something in the Greek or Hebrew, be sure to explain it in simple terms.

• **Use children's names and stories.** Listen for humorous family anecdotes and interject them whenever possible. Parents love to hear stories and kids enjoy the attention. If the material is sensitive, get permission first.

• **Make personal applications for children.** Talking about giving? Encourage children to tithe their allowances. Teaching about loving our enemies? Help kids understand this means bullies at school. Denouncing idol worship? Apply the lesson to video games, sports, or TV stars.

• **Let children help give the sermon.** Have children hold props, participate in illustrations, teach object lessons, or act out Bible stories.

CHAPTER 10

Reality Check

> "I am the Real Vine and my Father is the Farmer. He cuts off every branch of me that doesn't bear grapes. And every branch that is grape-bearing he prunes back so it will bear even more. You are already pruned back by the message I have spoken."
>
> (JOHN 15:1-3, *THE MESSAGE*)

I n the Margery Williams' classic, *The Velveteen Rabbit*, a trunk load of toys discover nursery magic and the art of becoming real. At the heart of the issue were mechanical toys who claimed superiority and arrogantly dismissed the other playthings. They even claimed to be real because they could move or even talk.

One day a rabbit, a Christmas gift and a new toy to the playroom, approached a wise old Skin Horse. The battered old horse was in terrible shape but somehow had withstood the test of time to remain a favorite plaything. The rabbit, curious about the Old Skin Horse's longevity and "realness," asked an insightful question:

"What is REAL?" asked the Rabbit one day, when they were lying side by side near the nursery fender, before Nana came to tidy the room. "Does it mean having things that buzz inside you and a stick-out handle?"

"Real isn't how you are made," said the Skin Horse. "It's a thing that happens to you. When a child loves you for a long, long time, not just to play with, but REALLY loves you, then you become Real."

"Does it hurt?" asked the Rabbit.

"Sometimes," said the Skin Horse, for he was always truthful. "When you are Real you don't mind being hurt."

"Does it happen all at once, like being wound up," he asked, "or bit by bit?"

"It doesn't happen all at once," said the Skin Horse. "You become. It takes a long time. That's why it doesn't happen often to people who break easily, or have sharp edges, or who have to be carefully kept. Generally, by the time you are Real, most of your hair has been loved off, and your eyes drop out and you get loose in the joints and very shabby. But these things don't matter at all, because once you are Real you can't be ugly, except to people who don't understand."[1]

Everybody seeks a real existence, even toys, according to this story.

When it comes to becoming the "real thing," smaller churches have an incredible edge. The small numbers allow for better intimacy and connection.

Ironically, God, in the form of Jesus, stepped down into our world and openly proclaimed himself as the "real" vine, as the only reality worth grafting one's life into. Jesus also taught that those who follow him and his teachings will recognize the truth and it will free them (John 8:32). This childhood story mirrors the reality of "becoming" Christ's disciple, of "becoming" his church, and of "becoming" his kingdom. Jesus is the real deal.

We definitely live in a culture that's captivated by reality. Reality TV—whether a game or nature show or how to build a bike—is all the rage. The Fox broadcasting company has a twenty-four-hour "all reality all the time" channel. And the most popular scripted dramas on TV are "real" (e.g., *24*, *CSI*).

Virtual reality has created a new postmodern question, similar to the velveteen rabbit's query: "What's real?" Our culture, like Pilate to Jesus, is screaming that question. A plastic world yearns for powerful experiences. A cyber culture is addicted to sensory overloads.

That's why the message of Jesus ("I am the true vine") is so attractive to postmodern culture. It's also the reason why the church has lost influence. In modern "churchianity" it's Halloween every day. We go to church and put on our masks. Our real worlds don't gel with our church life. After all, if people really knew the "real me" would they still connect or care? And it's not just with church that we masquerade, but also in our jobs and our homes. We get used to wearing masks.

One of the reasons our culture enjoys alcohol, drugs, and sexual activity is because these highs mask the pain. We want to "go where everyone knows our names" and forget real life. Unfortunately, these temporary buzzes fade and reality returns (often with a vengeance). For many believers, we make religion our drug and inject countless meetings and acts of ministry into our calendar. We seek one spiritual high after another in hopes we can feel free.

That's why I love smaller churches, especially the few that I came to find were like the Old Skin Horse. Loose in the joints. Severely worn. Missing parts. But in their fellowships I felt accepted and found support.

When it comes to becoming the "real thing," smaller churches have an incredible edge. The small numbers allow for better intimacy and connection (if cliques don't blind and bind). And a children's ministry that embraces reality and encourages real experiences with Jesus can frame a faith that recognizes temporary masks for what they are: empty Halloween charades. Authenticity will be a growing value in our postmodern culture. Can your church become "real"? Can your children's ministry forge an authentic Christian faith?

It's no secret recipe. And, trust me, any changes won't bring overnight success. Nevertheless, in regards to programming, evangelism, worship, fellowship activities, and Bible lessons, the answer is in approaching the situation with a R-E-A-L attitude: Is this *relevant?* Can it be *experienced?* How do we make this more *authentic?* And can we make it come to *life?* It's not "nursery magic" that will aid this process, but the transformative power of the Holy Spirit.

The very incarnation of Jesus (leaving Heaven as God to become a human) is an example of "becoming" relevant.

RELEVANT

The ability to build relevant bridges into the culture of children today is vital. Trust me, if you won't or can't, then social and cultural agencies will construct those crossings. Madison Avenue, Hollywood, and MTV seriously study kids to find what's making them tick, talk, and take. What are children consuming right now? What are their tastes?

Far too often the church is out of step with society and irrelevant. At best, we mimic culture and convert popular stuff into cute Christian mantras. The church has a reputation for being "unoriginal." We also like to target certain things to denounce. Harry Potter, the popular children's book series written by J. K. Rowling's, has been read by millions of children, including many church kids. The question for me is not whether Harry Potter is "evil," but how can I use Potter's world (including what may be evil) to help children see the cross of Christ? That's what it means to become relevant.

It's a biblical perspective that has been lost to many. The very incarnation of Jesus (leaving Heaven as God to become a human) is an example of "becoming" relevant. Jesus couldn't save man from Heaven. He had to become human to build the bridge. Ironically, Jesus was often accused by religious leaders as being worldly. He hung with whores, winos, and worse. But his participation did not mean he condoned their lifestyles. Rather, Jesus constantly encouraged the wicked to leave their lifestyles behind.

Paul also understood how to be relevant. In Acts 17, he enters the city of Athens and spends the day touring the city. He finds a culture, not unlike ours, filled with idols. How does Paul respond? Does he create faux paux Christian T-shirts that cleverly mimic the latest idol in fashion? Does he isolate himself in an Athenian home to avoid being stained? No, Paul eventually stands in the Areopagus and confronts the philosophers by quoting their own poets (Acts 17: 28) and challenging them to consider that an idol erected to an unknown God is just a temporary mask for reality. He then explains the real deal found in Jesus.

A relevant children's ministry will follow Jesus' and Paul's example. It will research popular kids' culture. Watch Nickelodeon and Disney. Go to a mall or Chuck E. Cheese's and just observe children at play. Listen to their comments. Ask the children in your ministry what they watch, listen to, or read. It may even mean reading Harry Potter (if that's what your children are into).

An authentic children's ministry starts by building the bridge into their culture. You can't reach them if you refuse to never enter their world.

EXPERIENTIAL

Just do it. Go for it. Get in the game. Get real. You are now free to move around the country.

The second force in creating an authentic children's ministry is to invest in experiential strategies. Our culture, especially children's, is wired towards the experiential. Children want to feel and taste and smell, not just hear and see. Video gaming is experiential. Guitar Hero allows kids to crawl inside the game to become a rock star. The popular Nintendo Wii gaming system literally recreates reality. With a palm controller, the gamer can bowl, swing a club, or turn a wheel. Wii is so close to reality that players complain of tennis elbows and bowlers' shoulders afterwards.

One of the first experiential amusement parks was Disneyland. It's an alternate reality where dreams come true "when you wish upon a star." Restaurants, like Chuck E. Cheese's and Rainforest Café, create a personal eating experience. Some of the most popular family getaways are experience-rich (e.g., Orlando, Las Vegas).

Unfortunately, the church has lost influence to a sensory-starved culture by focusing primarily upon sight and sound. Most church situations (including many children's programs) are passive, sit-and-soak experiences where lectures, sermons, and words rule. Even worship is watching someone perform on stage. The most experiential parts of a church service—Communion, baptisms, offerings—are reduced to minute-sized moments to be done out of tradition (weekly, monthly, or quarterly).

A children's ministry, especially in the smaller church, has powerful opportunity to reinvent church for children into powerful and personal experiences. The question is how do we become experiential? In part, it's done by moving beyond just eyes and ears alone. For example, in the popular worship song "Breathe," the lyrics proclaim that God is the "air we breathe" and in the chorus the song announces "I'm desperate for you." Instead of just singing that song, why not experience it? Encourage the children to try to hold their breath while the worship team sings the verse and then release it just as the chorus swells with "I'm desperate for you!" This experience is not only in line with the song's lyrical content, but also makes worship real.

The secret to becoming experiential is to check the "emotion quotient." The more the senses are tapped in an experience, the stronger the emotional response. Jesus was a master teacher who knew how to leave his audiences emotionally disturbed. The Pharisees left mad. Zacchaeus left glad. And the rich young ruler left sad. The deeper the emotions, the richer and more memorable the experience will be to the children. For example, I once had children put marbles in their shoes for a teaching experience. The pain of a stone in the sole helped illustrate the trouble sin impacts on one's real soul.

Smaller-church children's ministries have a wonderful advantage in using experiential worship, lessons, and activities because of their lower numbers. It's far easier to use experiential exercises with five or fifteen kids than fifty-five.

AUTHENTIC

Authenticity is an essential component to a real children's ministry. Recently, my family watched a movie where a scene incorporated computer imagery to replicate real animals doing some things real beasts don't normally do. It was a movie, but my son still said over and over how fake it seemed. In fact, in postmodern culture, that which is fake is also unbelievable (e.g., UFOs, Elvis sightings).

This presents a real challenge to the church in twenty-first century culture. After all, the gospel is, by its very virtue, an unbelievable piece of good news that must be believed though it seems too good to be true. A miracle, as recorded in the Scriptures, is inherently unbelievable and unnatural. People don't walk on water or find coins in a fish's mouth. For outsiders (and a lot of insiders too), church experiences often seem equally plastic and fake—even if our intentions are otherwise. I always find the "meet and greet" moment fascinating, especially as a visitor to a church. This is the moment when people who basically ignored me before—consciously or unconsciously—now are suddenly appreciative of my presence. Believe me, it sometimes comes off as fake.

In children's ministry we also run the risk of fakery when we resort to gimmicks (prizes, Bible Bucks, food) to bribe children to come to church, bring a Bible, or bring a friend. In these motivators, we unknowingly suggest trickery. What we offer isn't real enough to draw naturally, so we'll use a gimmick. For many children, what's really real about their church experience is not that they learned about Jesus, but that they discovered good works (bringing a friend or Bible or memorizing Scripture) really do earn rewards. Is that the message we want to send? I doubt it.

One Sunday school teacher answered a student's question about how the Bible and dinosaurs fit together with the absurd response that scientists actually invented fossils to prove evolutionary theory! Not only did this answer not satisfy the question, but ultimately it suggested that the church teacher didn't know what she was talking about. And if you couldn't trust her on dinosaurs, then why believe her teaching about Daniel? She's "lion" somehow. A far better answer would have been "I don't know. Let's figure that one out together."

Authentic children's ministry will also help children to understand biblical things by transforming the world of the Scripture into the child's world. For example, when teaching on the armor of God (Ephesians 6:10-18), give the passage an authentic charge by using football gear instead of Roman armor. Or if you want to truly authenticate a biblical story, truly get real. One children's ministry re-creates a real Passover meal for their children at Easter. The children taste lamb and bitter herbs and participate in rituals and recitations.

LIVING

A final force behind an authentic children's ministry is that it's alive and connective in nature. Children not only experience an authentic moment, but they also share that situation with others who can guide their interpretations about the experience.

A common complaint about church by those who don't attend is it's boring and dead. This criticism may sound hypersensitive at first, but there's some truth to the charge. If the good news (gospel) is really good news, then why is it so hard for 98 percent of Christians to share? Few individuals have trouble sharing their passion with others, whether it's a favorite sports team, song, or TV show. To not want to share their faith suggests that, for most Christians, Jesus isn't as "real" in their lives as these other activities.

Evangelism is a natural response, not a programmed activity. Revivals aren't events, but powerful and timely Holy Spirit-driven moments. If only the faithful few show for a revival service, something's deadly wrong. Why do most people—including church folk—find a Super Bowl party at a friend's home more appealing than Wednesday night Bible study? Could it be that one has more "life" enveloping it?

Ironically, as Christians we are "alive with Christ" (Ephesians 2:5). We are "living sacrifices" (Romans 12:1) who follow a "living Stone" (1 Peter 2:4). We have a "living hope" (1 Peter 1:3) through a "living way" (Hebrews 10:20) and have experienced rebirth by a "living . . . word" (1 Peter 1:23). And we have "living water" (John 7:38) in us that flows from us.

A children's ministry must connect kids to a living faith, not dying or dead traditions, rituals, or religiosity. The key is to ask yourself how alive are you in your faith? Does your faith work Monday through Saturday? Is it operating in the church hall as well as the local mall? Do children think of Jesus when they see you?

Is your heart passionately pursuing the things of God? Does your soul break when you see kids captured by greed, captivated by worldly voices, or caught by sin?

Are your classrooms, your meetings, and your events dry and boring places? Do you secretly wish you could slip out or skip altogether? Do you look forward to teaching or does the thought of another Sunday lesson bore even you?

Many smaller-church children's ministries are woefully addicted to mediocrity and their "aliveness" quotient is barely registering any life at all (sometimes reflective of a greater church deadness). Such ministries will not attract children or their parents. A dead faith is unappealing.

This may be the only area of the four that requires a Holy Spirit charging. It's not hard to reinvent lessons into something more experiential. It's not difficult to be more relevant if we choose. It's easy to create more authentic moments. But only the Holy Spirit can breathe life. The real deal is a change from within.

REALITY CHECKS

Ultimately, a smaller-church children's ministry must constantly invite reality checks. It must regularly evaluate its programming, its staff, and its vision for aliveness. What's real? What's true?

And while the Holy Spirit can work miracles instantaneously, much of this becoming real doesn't happen overnight. It doesn't work with people who can't handle the messy, goofy, and gross culture that children live in today. Becoming real will also hurt. Some people won't understand. Others will criticize, even condemn.

But the truth is it's far worse to be dead in a living faith. And the smaller church is a ripe place for life and death. But like Joshua, we'll only see walls fall and enemies routed when we choose to serve a Living God over idols and false worship. We won't find life in a canned program, a packaged philosophy, or a book (including this one). These things are only means to the end. When we idolize a larger church's ideas, imitate another's programming, or deify someone's insights—no matter how deep—we stand in the way of God working distinctly and uniquely in our church.

It's time to let God breathe life into your children's ministry. Become real. Choose authenticity. Build positive, powerful, and personal experiences. Seek relevant bridges into the lives of children. Ask God to bless your plans and always be open to fresh winds of the Spirit.

To breathe is to be real.

To be real is to be alive.

To be alive is to be divine.

To be divine is to be whole.

Reality Check

Use this worksheet to evaluate how REAL your children's ministry is.

Relevant

What are your children consuming right now? What are their tastes? How are you building bridges into their world?

Experiential

What have you done recently to make worship real for kids? What is the "emotion quotient" in the programming you provide?

Authentic

How often do you resort to using gimmicks in your children's ministry? Are teachers answering kids' questions honestly? What do you do to help kids understand the Bible on their level?

Living

How alive are you in your faith? How is the Holy Spirit helping you communicate the gospel with life and excitement?

AFTERWORD

So here we are at the end. I hope our journey together has been a blessing. I can tell you, as I poured over each word, insight, idea, and application I tried to keep you in mind. I imagined your heartaches, your joys, and your frustrations. Hopefully, as you read the pages, you found yourself within the lines.

I truly do love the smaller church. And I enjoy watching God work through the small things. A boy's lunch. A mustard seed. A motley crew of Galilean disciples. What the world calls insignificant, God can mold to change the world. What the world believes lacks value, God can give the golden touch.

Just remember that if you think small, you'll get small.

You're a smaller church, true. But you're not small in God's providential care. It's been said the last seven words of a dying church are "we've never done it that way before." That's why you can't allow methods to become monuments. If you're still doing children's ministry the same way as last year or five years ago or twenty years ago, you're irrelevant.

People love fresh bread. So relax and rely upon God. You may never grow larger in number, but that doesn't mean you can't grow larger in influence. What do you want your children to remember about their church experience? Maybe it's time to change, charge, or challenge. Maybe it's time to listen, learn, or love.

I'll be honest, I can't think of a final word for this book. I don't know how to end a journey that's still incomplete in my mind. You may still have questions. And I know I still have unwritten thoughts. So let me close by inviting you to write me. I'd love to hear your story and, if time allows, respond to any lingering question you might possess.

I care.

Rick

Contact e-mail: rickchromey@juno.com

ENDNOTES

INTRODUCTION
[1] *Transforming Children into Spiritual Champions: Why Children Should Be Your Church's #1 Priority* (Ventura, CA: Gospel Light, 2003), 34.

[2] The Barna Report. "Small Churches Struggle to Grow Because of the People They Attract," September 2, 2003. http://www.barna.org/FlexPage.aspx?Page=BarnaUpdate&BarnaUpdateID=148. Accessed July 29, 2007.

CHAPTER 1
[1] George Barna, *User-Friendly Churches* (Ventura, CA; Regal Books, 1991), 24.

[2] Ibid., 124.

CHAPTER 2
[1] As quoted by Jimmy Long, *Emerging Hope: A Strategy for Reaching Postmoderns* (Downers Grove: InterVarsity Press, 2004), 20.

[2] Leonard Sweet, *Carpe Mañana* (Grand Rapids: Zondervan, 2001), 8.

[3] John Naisbitt, *High Tech, High Tough: Technology and Our Search for Meaning* (New York: Broadway Books, 1000), 25–26.

[4] Ibid., 26.

[5] Ibid., 3.

[6] A term coined by the philosopher Charles Sanders Pierce. Leonard Sweet and Brian McLaren, *A Is for Abductive: The Language of the Emerging Church* (Grand Rapids: Zondervan, 2003), 31.

CHAPTER 4
[1] *The Perfect Thing: How the iPod Shuffles Commerce, Culture and Coolness* by Steven Levy (New York, NY: Simon Schuster, 2006), 81.

[2] Ibid., 92.

[3] Ibid., 118.

[4] Ibid., 93.

[5] *The Power of Vision* by George Barna (Ventura, CA: Regal Books, 1992), 122-129.

CHAPTER 8

[1]*"Young Adults Aren't Sticking with Church,"* by Cathy Lynn Grossman, USA Today Online. http://www.usatoday.com/news/religion/2007-08-06-church-dropouts_N.htm?csp=34   Accessed August 15, 2007.

[2]*They Like Jesus, but Not the Church: Insights from Emerging Generations* by Dan Kimball (Grand Rapids, MI: Zondervan, 2007): 16.

[3]"Young Adults Aren't Sticking." http://www.usatoday.com/news/religion/2007-08-06-church-dropouts_N.htm?csp=34

CHAPTER 10

[1] Margery Williams, The Velveteen Rabbit: Or How Toys Become Real. Garden City, NY: Doubleday and Company, Inc. Accessed online September 2, 2007. http://digital.library.upenn.edu/women/williams/rabbit/rabbit.html

DR. RICK CHROMEY serves on the staff at George Fox University (Boise Center) in Idaho. Previously he served as a youth and family ministry professor for Kentucky Christian University, Saint Louis Christian College, and Boise Bible College. He is also a professional consultant and trainer for several organizations, with a specialty in children's ministry.

Chromey earned a doctorate from George Fox Seminary (D.Min., Leadership in the Emerging Culture) in 2007 and is also a graduate of Nebraska Christian College (BSc., 1986) and Cincinnati Christian University (M.R.E., 1992).

He has previously authored two books, *Youth Ministry in Small Churches* (1990) and *The Children's Ministry Guide to the Smaller Church* (1995), and contributed to several works, including *The Youth Bible* and *Children's Ministry in the 21st Century* (Group 2006). He is frequently published in *Christian Standard* and *Children's Ministry Magazine* (where he currently pens the Ages 10-12 Insights column).

Rick enjoys spending time with his family, traveling, music, and motorcycles.

escn
energizing smaller churches network

about the escn

The Energizing Smaller Churches Network (ESCN) promotes the health and growth of smaller churches by affirming their value and enlarging their vision.

Formed by a group of church leaders with a burden to help smaller churches achieve their ministry potential, the ESCN has experienced significant growth since its inception in 2004.

In addition to the popular ESCN conferences for smaller churches held across the nation, the ESCN is a true network, bringing together leaders and volunteers in smaller churches across America through special programs, Internet communication, consultation, and relationship building. For more information go to www.escnetwork.com.

Also available from Standard Publishing:

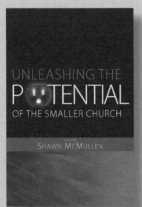

Unleashing the Potential of the Smaller Church
9780784716212

Releasing the Power of the Smaller Church
9780784721469

edited by Shawn McMullen

To order visit your local Christian bookstore, go online at www.standardpub.com, or call 1-800-543-1353.